# The Psychoanalytic Understanding of Consciousness, Free Will, Language, and Reason

*The Psychoanalytic Understanding of Consciousness, Free Will, Language, and Reason* examines the ways in which we can use psychoanalysis in order to better understand humanity and explores the question of what makes us human.

For thousands of years, thinkers have been trying to define what makes us human. Some of the main questions they have asked is: What is consciousness? Do we have free will? Do animals use language? And what does reason mean? Samuels argues that we need to better understand the psychoanalytic approach to human nature in order to answer these questions, as well as using it to provide a new way of understanding issues such as addiction, political conflict, ideology, and destructive personal relationship.

This book will be of vital interest to psychotherapists, as well as students and researchers across the fields of psychoanalysis, philosophy, and psychology.

**Robert Samuels, PhD**, holds doctorates in psychology and English, and teaches at the University of California, Santa Barbara. Among his many books are *Freud for the Twenty-First Century*, *Psychoanalyzing the Left and Right after Donald Trump*, *Between Philosophy and Psychoanalysis: Lacan's Reconstruction of Freud*, *Hitchcock's Bi-Textuality*, and *The Psychopathology of Political Ideologies*.

## Comparative Psychoanalysis Book Series
Series Editors: David Henderson and Jon Mills

*Comparative Psychoanalysis* studies controversy and dialogue in psychoanalysis. Intellectual, personal, and institutional conflict are endemic to the history of psychoanalysis. Alongside this there are creative efforts to establish understanding and communication among differing perspectives. Comparative methodologies are encouraged among all schools of psychoanalysis regardless of topic, theoretical or clinical orientation, or application to the behavioral sciences and humanities including historical reassessments, conceptual clarification, clinical exploration, reflections on the future of applied psychoanalytic thought, and attempts to articulate the conditions for fruitful dialogue. All subject matters in the arts and humanities, philosophy, anthropology, cultural studies, and the human sciences are ripe for comparative investigation within the frameworks of theoretical, clinical, and applied psychoanalysis. As an inherently interdisciplinary field of study, psychoanalysis requires a robust understanding of comparative methodology. Controversial discussions and criticism are invited. In the spirit of pluralism, Comparative Psychoanalysis is open to any theoretical school in the history of the psychoanalytic movement that offers novel critique, integration, and important insights in comparative scholarship.

# The Psychoanalytic Understanding of Consciousness, Free Will, Language, and Reason

## What Makes Us Human?

Robert Samuels

R Routledge
Taylor & Francis Group

LONDON AND NEW YORK

Designed cover image: © Getty Images

First published 2023
by Routledge
4 Park Square, Milton Park, Abingdon, Oxon OX14 4RN

and by Routledge
605 Third Avenue, New York, NY 10158

*Routledge is an imprint of the Taylor & Francis Group, an informa business*

© 2023 Robert Samuels

*British Library Cataloguing-in-Publication Data*
A catalogue record for this book is available from the British Library

ISBN: 978-1-032-42861-1 (hbk)
ISBN: 978-1-032-42860-4 (pbk)
ISBN: 978-1-003-36461-0 (ebk)

DOI: 10.4324/9781003364610

Typeset in Times New Roman
by MPS Limited, Dehradun

This book is dedicated to two great humans, Madeleine and Sophia

# Contents

# Chapter 1

# Introduction

For thousands of years, thinkers have been trying to define what makes us human. Some of the main questions they have asked is: What is consciousness? Do we have free will? Do animals use language? And what does reason mean?[1] This book argues that philosophers, neuroscientists, and evolutionary psychologists have been unable to answer these questions because they do not understand the psychoanalytic approach to human nature. This lack of comprehension results in false claims and half-truths about what it means to be human, and so I hope this book provides a better sense of our humanity. Moreover, this analysis is not just a purely academic exercise since our ability to protect our climate and pursue human rights is predicated on our clear understanding of what it means to be human.

One might ask why psychoanalysis is given such a privileged place in this vital discussion, and the main reason is that Freud was able to think about these core issues in an open and creative way that avoided traditional definitions of mental functioning. His openness allowed him to document four radical breaks that help define what makes us different from other animals. The first break that he presented was through his theory of consciousness and his realization that thought allows humans to escape from reality as they become immersed in fictional representations of the real world.[2] In fact, it was by analyzing his own dreams that he first discovered the way we are able to confuse memories and perceptions. He then made the leap to create an equivalence between the dream state, psychosis, animistic cultures, and thought itself.[3] For Freud, consciousness cannot be separated from psychosis because as Descartes insists, we never know when we are thinking if we are awake or experiencing a dream.[4] Not only does this theory of consciousness mean that the mind can transcend matter, but on the level of thought itself, we cannot distinguish between fiction and reality. Thus, one of the things that makes humans unique is our ability to hallucinate a false reality, and therefore we are able to break free from our immersion in the material world.[5]

For philosophers and neuroscientists, one of the key questions is how do we move from the physical materiality of the brain to mental states that go beyond the physical world.[6] Freud's theory of consciousness answers this

DOI: 10.4324/9781003364610-1

question by showing how our ability to hallucinate and imagine allows us the chance to jump from the material to the psychological. On its most basic level, Freud posits that we spontaneously combine memories with perceptions, and this mixture equates inner thoughts with the perception of external reality.[7] According to Freud, psychotics, infants, animistic cultures, and dreamers, all experience their thoughts as if they are coming from the outside material world. So if we want to understand what consciousness and perception is, we have to first realize that hallucination is our primary experience of the world.

The second major break that Freud helps to introduce is through his theory of sexuality.[8] By arguing that human sexuality is not driven by the evolutionary goal of reproduction, Freud helps us to see how humans make a break with nature and biology. Due to the fact that we can replace the objects of our instincts, we are not born pre-wired like other animals. Freud insists that our sexuality is perverse because anything can become sexualized, and people react to sex with both horror and excitement. This theory of sexuality also tells us that since we are not defined by our instincts or biology, we have the possibility of free will. As psychoanalysis insists, our drives are always partial, and so there is a gap in our being that opens the door for human difference and what psychoanalysis calls desire, and since we have free will and desire, we are able to influence our lives in ways that other animals cannot achieve.[9]

Paradoxically, one way to think about human free will is to look at addictions, which show that we can become invested in the pursuit of external objects to such an extent that we can destroy ourselves.[10] As a human drive, an addiction provides an escape not only from biological nature but also from self-interest and social necessity. We are thus free to desire what we want, but our fixation on these arbitrary objects leads us to seek immediate gratification and to avoid all social restrictions. Freud explains these drives through his theory of the pleasure principle, which claims that we are driven to escape tension, conflict, and reality through the immediate access to enjoyment.[11] It is therefore misleading to call addictions "diseases" because they are not primarily biological; instead, addictions represent a gap in our instincts, and this gap opens us up to becoming fixated on different objects than other animals.

Besides consciousness and free will, another problem for philosophers and neuroscientists is the question of whether other animals have language.[12] One reason it is so hard for people to answer this question is that they do not understand the contradictory nature of human representation: human language combines being with non-being and the self with the other.[13] As Hegel argues, I can say "I," but so can anyone else, and this means that this primary signifier is both universal and singular.[14] In other words, language allows us the ability to escape from the law of non-contradiction as we are able to be both something and its opposite at the same time.[15]

Freud first discovered this contradictory nature of human language when he was working with hysterical patients who presented symptoms that did not make biological or logical sense.[16] For instance, a patient would be unable to use her hand, but there was no biological explanation for this disorder; instead, Freud found that the patient was able to convert mental memories into physical signs, but due to the process of repression, the patient had no awareness of this symbolic substitution.[17] In fact, it is the theory of repression that is so hard for many philosophers and neuroscientists to understand because they do not accept that a person can lie to himself or herself.[18] After all, if there is anything we know, it is our own thoughts, but psychoanalysis tells us that we do not know ourselves, and we have the ability to break with biological and mental causality since we can always displace and replace our memories.[19] The psychoanalytic view of memory is dynamic and recursive, which means that we are constantly changing our memories by placing them in a network of other memories, and due to the mental autonomy of human thinking, these memories can be either true or false.[20]

In his "Project for a Scientific Psychology," Freud makes another important leap by seeing neurons as a set of symbols connected together in a network of associations.[21] Memories are then not physical or biological entities; rather, they are signs related to other signs in an emerging system that has no beginning or end or stable presence. Not only does this theory of memory show how we structure our inner experience, but it also reveals how our social relations are also structured through language and symbolic associations.[22] While some other primates do have social hierarchies and a primitive form of communication, they do not have symbolic memories and symbolic social systems. It is important to stress that a symbol is something that represents something else, and so it is defined by its contradictory nature.

Just as every word relates to other words, every person is defined by their relation to other people. Identity is therefore based on difference, and people only know themselves by comparing themselves to others.[23] Our social being is then centered on the ability of language to combine opposites and place differences in a network of retained associations. This theory of language is so hard for philosophers and neuroscientists to think because it goes against the law of non-contradiction, and it is founded on the differential nature of symbolic representations.

In addition to this rethinking of free will, consciousness, and language, psychoanalysis also pushes us to ask what is reason? For Freud, a key move was to realize that thought itself allowed people to escape from perceiving reality, and so humans have to learn how to limit their thinking and to accept that not everything can be known. Similar to Kant's idea that we cannot know the thing-in-itself, but we can understand how we think about reality, Freud developed his theory of the reality principle to explain how we can use reason to approach truth if we first learn how to remove our own

investments in our memories and thoughts.[24] Just as Descartes posits that
we have to give up all bias and assumptions in order to apply reason in a
scientific manner, Freud argues that we need to apply the reality principle by
separating our memories from our perceptions of the external world.[25]
Through a process of dis-investment, we learn how to be disinterested judges
of our own experiences. In short, reason is reality testing, which itself
requires critical self-analysis and a break with the pleasure principle.

Another aspect of reason is that it must also cut its ties with the subjective
dependency on others. For Freud, transference relates to the way that we
seek to escape from our own helplessness and freedom by transferring
responsibility onto others.[26] For Freud, the roots of the transference are
derived from the cry of the baby and the response of the care-taker.[27] When
a baby cries, it is making a demand to the Other for love, recognition, and
knowledge, but this demand can never be totally fulfilled.[28] Moreover,
Freud argues that the demand makes the helpless child dependent on the
powerful adult, and therefore all social and linguistic relationships derive
their foundation from this initial request for the other to make all suffering
and dis-pleasure go away.[29]

In *Totem and Taboo*, Freud posited that at the heart of all religions is a
demand (prayer) made to an imaginary Other, and what then allows science
to emerge is a giving up of this demand so that one no longer transfers
power and responsibility onto others. Freedom and reason are then achieved
when we move beyond transference, and we realize that there is no one or
nothing that is going to make all of our suffering disappear. In fact, psychoanalysis, as a practice of radical self-honesty, does not eliminate the
fundamental conflicts between culture and nature or society and the individual; rather, psychoanalysis is dedicated to freely examining the effects of
these unresolvable differences.[30] Other approaches cannot accomplish this
level of truth because they seek to avoid or resolve the fundamental conflicts
shaping human existence.

To further elucidate how psychoanalysis differs from other perspectives, I
will begin by looking at the television series *Westworld* to determine why
humans are not purely animals or machines. While this show does a good
job at asking the question of what makes us human, it ultimately provides
the wrong answers because it does not comprehend the psychoanalytic
perspective on sexuality, consciousness, language, and reason. However, the
program is still helpful since it clarifies some of the stakes involved in determining the difference between humans and machines and the role culture
plays in hiding this conflict.

Chapter Three looks at Sam Harris' book *The Moral Land*scape to examine the different ways neuroscience and evolutionary psychology block
our ability to understand what makes us human.[31] In trying to establish a
science of morality, Harris ends up producing a repression of psychoanalysis
and the establishment of a totalizing form of scientism.[32] There are also

profound political implications to this replacement of psychoanalysis with biological determinism.

In Chapter Four, I turn to Steven Pinker's *The Language Instinct*. We shall see that his reliance on evolutionary psychology and neuro-biology prevents him from seeing how humans are not determined by their instincts.[33] Furthermore, because he fails to recognize the ways human consciousness transcends material reality, he is unable to determine what differentiates humans from animals. This lack of distinction leads him to make the common mistake of comparing human beings to language processing machines. What he then misses is the way that our relationship to others is predicated on an unconscious demand for love, recognition, and knowledge within the structure of transference. Pinker also does not define reason as the separation of memory from perception and what Freud calls the limitations of our own knowledge in the face of an unknowable real.

Chapter Five examines Daniel Dennett's *From Bacteria to Bach and Back* to further explore what people get wrong about the uniqueness of human beings.[34] Like Pinker, Dennett turns to evolutionary theory in order to explain how we are shaped by biology, and why we are not very different from other animals. He also combines together computer science and evolutionary psychology to wrongly assert that we are fundamentally information processing machines. By confusing DNA with digital code, Dennett asserts that we are computers pre-programmed through natural selection.

Chapter Six then looks at why so many psychoanalysts tend to misunderstand what makes us human. Through an analysis of Mark Solms' work, I reveal the problem of trying to combine psychoanalysis and neuroscience.[35] Since I argue in this book that psychoanalysis offers us the best way to understand what makes us human, it is important to look at the ways people from within the field repress its most radical insights. It will be my argument that there is a common misunderstanding of reason, consciousness, drives, language, transference, and free association, and if we do not clarify these confusions, we will not be able to see how psychoanalysis differs from other approaches in its response to the quest of defining our common humanity.

Chapter Seven examines Jordan Peterson's *12 Rules for Life*, which offers an interesting mix of Jungian philosophy, evolutionary psychology, and Christian theology. Like so many of the writers and theorists discussed in this work, Peterson tends to erase the difference between humans and other animals. This repression of what makes us human is often tied to his return to traditional social hierarchies, prejudices, and stereotypes. For instance, he equates humans to lobsters in order to show how cultural and psychological dominance is based on biological determinism.

The final chapter answers the question of why it is important to know what makes us human. It turns out that the only way we can begin to know ourselves and our world is if we fully comprehend why we are neither computers nor animals. Therefore, if we want to build a more just and sustainable world, we have to be able to fully grasp human reason, and this process requires a deeper understanding of human sexuality, thought, and language. Moreover, it is only psychoanalysis that can provide the path to this understanding.

## Notes

1 Chalmers, David. "The Hard Problem of Consciousness." *The Blackwell Companion to Consciousness,* 2007. 225–235.
2 Freud, Sigmund, and A. J. Cronin. *The Interpretation of Dreams.* Read Books, 2013.
3 Freud, Sigmund, and Anna Freud. *Totem and Taboo and Other Works.* Vol. 13. Random House, 2001.
4 Descartes, René. *Discourse on Method and the Meditations.* Penguin UK, 1968.
5 Samuels, Robert. "The Unconscious and the Primary Processes." *Freud for the Twenty-First Century.* Palgrave Pivot, Cham, 2019. 27–42.
6 Dennett, Daniel C. *From Bacteria to Bach and back: The Evolution of Minds.* WW Norton, 2017.
7 Freud, Sigmund. "Project for a Scientific Psychology (1950 [1895])." *The Standard Edition of the Complete Psychological Works of Sigmund Freud, Volume I (1886–1899): Pre-Psycho-Analytic Publications and Unpublished Drafts,* 1966. 281–391.
8 Freud, Sigmund. *Three Essays on the Theory of Sexuality: The 1905 Edition.* Verso Books, 2017.
9 Boothby, Richard. *Death and Desire (RLE: Lacan): Psychoanalytic Theory in Lacan's Return to Freud.* Routledge, 2014.
10 Baldwin, Yael Goldman. *Lacan and Addiction: An Anthology.* Routledge, 2018.
11 Freud, Sigmund. *Beyond the Pleasure Principle.* Penguin UK, 2003.
12 Premack, David. "Words: What Are They, and Do Animals Have Them?." *Cognition* 37.3 (1990): 197–212.
13 Lacan, Jacques. "The Function and Field of Speech and Language in Psychoanalysis." *Écrits: A Selection,* 1977. 30–113.
14 Hegel, Georg Wilhelm Friedrich. *Hegel: The Phenomenology of Spirit.* Oxford University Press, 2018.
15 Pippin, Robert B. "Hegel's Metaphysics and the Problem of Contradiction." *Journal of the History of Philosophy* 16.3 (1978): 301–312.
16 Freud, Sigmund. "Hysterical Phantasies and Their Relation to Bisexuality." *The Standard Edition of the Complete Psychological Works of Sigmund Freud, Volume IX (1906–1908): Jensen's 'Gradiva'and Other Works,* 1959. 155–166.
17 Freud, Sigmund. "A Case of Successful Treatment by Hypnotism: With Some Remarks on the Origin of Hysterical Symptoms Through 'Counter-Will.'" *The Standard Edition of the Complete Psychological Works of Sigmund Freud, Volume I (1886–1899): Pre-Psycho-Analytic Publications and Unpublished Drafts,* 1966. 115–128.
18 Anderson, Michael C. "Repression: A Cognitive Neuroscience Approach." *Psychoanalysis and Neuroscience.* Springer, Milano, 2006. 327–349.
19 Freud, Sigmund. "Project for a Scientific Psychology (1950 [1895])." *The Standard Edition of the Complete Psychological Works of Sigmund Freud, Volume I (1886–1899): Pre-Psycho-Analytic Publications and Unpublished Drafts,* 1966. 281–391.

20 Lacan, Jacques, Jacques-Alain Ed Miller, and Russell Trans Grigg. "The Seminar of Jacques Lacan, Book 3: The Psychoses 1955–1956." *Translation of the Seminar that Lacan Delivered to the Société Française de Psychoanalyse over the Curse of the Academic Year 1955–1956.* WW Norton, 1993.
21 Samuels, Robert. "Pathos, Hysteria, and the Left." *Zizek and the Rhetorical Unconscious.* Palgrave Macmillan, Cham, 2020. 33–47.
22 Miller, Jacques-Alain, Paul Verhaeghe, and Ellie Ragland. *Jacques Lacan and the Other Side of Psychoanalysis: Reflections on Seminar XVII, sic vi.* Vol. 6. Duke University Press, 2006.
23 Lacan, Jacques. *The Seminar of Jacques Lacan: The Ego in Freud's Theory and in the Technique of Psychoanalysis 1954–1955/Transl. by Sylvana Tomaselli.* Cambridge University Press, 1988.
24 Freud, Sigmund. "Negation." *Organization and Pathology of Thought: Selected Sources.* Columbia University Press, 1951. 338–348.
25 Samuels, Robert. "Science and the Reality Principle." *Freud for the Twenty-First Century.* Palgrave Pivot, Cham, 2019. 5–16.
26 Freud, Sigmund. "The Dynamics of Transference." *The Standard Edition of the Complete Psychological Works of Sigmund Freud, Volume XII (1911–1913): The Case of Schreber, Papers on Technique and Other Works,* 1958. 97–108.
27 Samuels, Robert. "Transference and Narcissism." *Freud for the Twenty-First Century.* Palgrave Pivot, Cham, 2019. 43–51.
28 Lacan, Jacques. "The Subversion of the Subject and the Dialectic of Desire in the Freudian Unconscious." *Hegel and Contemporary Continental Philosophy* 19.6 (1960): 205–235.
29 Freud, Sigmund. "Project for a Scientific Psychology (1950 [1895])." *The Standard Edition of the Complete Psychological Works of Sigmund Freud, Volume I (1886–1899): Pre-Psycho-Analytic Publications and Unpublished Drafts,* 1966. 281–391.
30 Rieff, Philip. *Freud: The Mind of the Moralist.* University of Chicago Press, 1979.
31 Harris, Sam. *The Moral Landscape: How Science Can Determine Human Values.* Simon and Schuster, 2011.
32 Stenmark, Mikael. *Scientism: Science, Ethics and Religion.* Routledge, 2017.
33 Pinker, Steven. *The Language Instinct: How the Mind Creates Language.* Penguin UK, 2003.
34 Dennett, Daniel C. *From Bacteria to Bach and Back: The Evolution of Minds.* WW Norton, 2017.
35 Solms, Mark. *The Feeling Brain: Selected Papers on Neuropsychoanalysis.* Routledge, 2018.

# Chapter 2

# Psychoanalyzing *Westworld*: Beyond Robots and Computers

The television show *Westworld* pushes us to ask what makes us human and how do we define free well and consciousness? If we think of the first season as a thought experiment seeking to define the human, then we must turn to psychoanalysis to answer these questions because only this discipline presents an accurate theorizing of the central aspects of human existence. It turns out that a key to this psychoanalytic approach is the production of several anti-intuitive threshold concepts: drives, consciousness, transference, and neutrality.[1] As we shall see, each one of these notions is determined by an interplay between lack and excess.

## Drives

As Lacan stresses, humans are not completely controlled by their instincts because there is a gap in our biology and evolution. In focusing on the partiality of drives, psychoanalysis allows us to see that we are unlike any other animal since our instincts are open and only partly dictate our actions.[2] For instance, Freud reveals that since the object of our drives can be substituted and displaced, anything can become a source of satisfaction.[3] In other words, the lack of biological determination opens up a space for an excess of sexualization. Since there is no natural connection between the subject and the object of a drive, every drive can be subverted and perverted. Freud presents this unnatural relation to nature through his theories of sexuality and the separation of sexuality from biological reproduction.

Most other theories of what makes us human thus fail because they do not fully affirm the openness and variability of human drives. This break from biology and evolution calls into question evolutionary psychology and neuroscience, which tend to rely on a strict causality between a biological cause and a human effect.[4] However, for Lacan, the human subject is a discontinuity in the Real, and this means that there is always a gap between any cause and effect.[5]

DOI: 10.4324/9781003364610-2

## Thought

The second major break for the human revolves around the concept of consciousness. Like Descartes, Freud argues that thoughts are not grounded in reality.[6] In fact, right before Descartes states his famous "I think, therefore, I am," he relates that he does not know if he is awake or dreaming, and therefore humans never know for sure if they are living in a real or fictious world.[7] Descartes adds that he can imagine not having a body or living in an imaginary world, but he cannot imagine not thinking in both the real and fictional worlds. Yet, Descartes seeks to rescue his "I" by tying his thought to his being, but it should be clear that in the dream state, there is no "I" or ego controlling our representations.[8]

Freud adds that in the dream state, psychotic hallucination, and primitive animism, memories are confused with the perception of the external world, and so on the level of human consciousness, there can be no reality testing.[9] Humans thus have the ability to escape the material world and experience automatic fictions. If people are conscious of their dreams and their hallucinations, we have to affirm that consciousness and the feeling of having a unique experience are not purely rational or intentional.

## Transference

Another key concept that is hard for psychologists, philosophers, and neuroscientists to accept is the notion of transference. This concept not only explains how we become alienated through identification with others, but it also defines our fundamental relationship to other people.[10] Lacan demonstrates how all humans are born premature since it takes us a very long time compared to other animals to gain control over our bodies.[11] This lack of coordination is coupled with an excess because the way we gain a sense of having a coherent body and self is by identifying with an ideal external image in the mirror or another person around the same size and age. This image acts as a gestalt since its whole is greater than the sum of its pieces.[12] In other words, our relation to our body is not natural or material; rather we have a virtual relation with our body. After all, we can never see all of our body at once, and so we are forced to imagine its unity and coherence.

For Freud, the virtual nature of the body was first discovered when he encountered hysterical patients who had symptoms that did not make anatomical sense.[13] For instance, a woman would be able to use her hand, but she could not use other parts of her arm. The hysterical symptom, then, represents a break with anatomical causality, but it also represents a break with psychological causality since the hysteric does not know the origin of the symptom.[14] In turn, this lack of causality, threatens the doctor and the scientist because it undermines their intuitive understanding of cause and effect. It is important to stress that Freud first uses the term *transference* to point to the way hysterics displace the affect of one memory onto another memory.[15] This transference of affect is often coupled with a substitution of bodily signifiers so that the feelings associated with one part of the body gets replaced with sensations caused by another body part.[16]

The subject's prematurity also results in a transference of responsibility from the self to the other. Freud believed that when an infant first encounters an unmet need, the first response is to activate the primary processes and hallucinate a scene of satisfaction.[17] Later, when this process still leaves the subject unsatisfied, the child cries hoping to get the other to make the lack go away. For Freud, this cry to the Other represents the foundation of human communication, empathy, and understanding. In other words, the helplessness of the child produces an excess of dependency that structures social relations. Transference, then, embodies our demand that the Other resolve our problems by giving us love, knowledge, and recognition.[18] In turn, the psychoanalytic process requires an optimal frustration of this insatiable demand.

For Lacan, transference is determined by a process of deception where the patient idealizes the Other so that the other will idealize the patient. In the structure of obsessional narcissism, I become an other for the Other since I want to have my ideal self recognized by an ideal Other.[19] The unconscious goal of this process is to escape feelings of guilt, shame, and responsibility. In other words, I seek to escape my own freedom by creating an ideal Other who is responsible for everything.[20] We see this process in action when Descartes turns to god as the one who guarantees truth and the order of the world.[21] Once again, in this act of transference, the human makes a break with reality testing and invests in a process of self-deception.

## Neutrality

The fourth level of human difference involves the ability to take a neutral perspective on internal and external reality. For Freud, the reality principle requires a de-cathexis of desire and an acceptance of the limitation of thinking.[22] We must learn how to accept the loss of objects and the giving up of our investments. In Descartes' case, he centers modern science on the introspective process of moving beyond bias and self-interest.[23] On the level of modern science, we have to learn to become impartial judges of empirical reality, but we must mediate this relation to the Real through the use of logic and math. Reason then becomes a necessary but impossible ideal centered on universality, neutrality, and objectivity.[24] Moreover, as Hegel highlights, we need to abstract ourselves from our immediate environment and social world in order to apply universal reason to inner and outer nature.[25]

This break from immediacy differentiates us from other animals and opens the door for social practices and social institutions that are not based on evolution or some natural order. Moreover, Descartes ties the universal ability to reason to the foundations of modern democracy since there is no need to depend on a single source of authority or meaning if we all have the potential to discover truth through our own logic and unbiased experience.[26] Thus, a challenge for evolutionary biology, psychology, computer science, and neuroscience is how to think about social practices that combine the freedom of the individual with necessary but impossible ideals.[27] We have free will then because we can remove ourselves from nature and our dependency on others.

## Entering *Westworld*

To explore these fundamental psychoanalytic contributions to what makes us human, I want to look at what season one of *Westworld* gets wrong and what it gets right.[28] A central theme of the show is to ponder not only what makes us human but to also ask if it is possible to create robots that are indistinguishable from humans?[29] Although, I will not focus on the latter question, it is important to stress that this media production presents an extreme form of what already exists in the world of artificial intelligence. Instead of determining whether it will be possible to construct robots that appear to be human, I will examine the way the series misunderstands humanity.

It is interesting that the first lines of the first episode directly address psychoanalysis. In this scene, the programmer/robot Bernard asks the robot (host) Dolores if she knows where she is, and she replies that she is in a dream. He then asks her if she ever questions the nature of her reality, and she answers by saying no. According to the logic of the show, the best way to stop the robots from rebelling is to tell them that they are living in a dream state, and thus, there is no reason to apply the reality principle and question their own internal nature.[30] Of course, we have no reason to believe that intelligent machines will ever be able to dream or have an unconscious, but the interesting twist here is to use the dream state as a place where one stops questioning the reality of one's inner and outer world.[31]

As I argued earlier, for Freud, dreams are a primary process in the unconscious that confuse internal representations with the perception of the external world, and not only does this process suspend reality testing but it also removes the self from its own representations. Paradoxically, the best way to define human consciousness is the effect of this break from both the material world and the intentional self.[32]

From the perspective of evolutionary psychology, we should be able to determine how our ability to be conscious helps us to survive and reproduce.[33] One possible explanation revolves around Freud's idea that thoughts are experimental actions, and so we can test reality by imagining the effects of certain actions and risks in a safe realm.[34] However, we also know that dreams represent a break from the reality principle and material determinism. Perhaps we dream so that we can satisfy our desires without having to spend much physical energy on accessing satisfaction in reality. Ultimately, the question of cause is less important from a psychoanalytic perspective since its worldview is predicated on a break with material causality.

## Cultural Fantasy

Within the context of *Westworld,* a central theme is the roles played by fantasy and other imaginary cultural spaces in human desire and self-consciousness.[35] When people enter the alternative reality of the park, they seek to discover their true selves by accessing their primal sexual and violent impulses, which have been repressed and contained by social dictates.[36] Like a dream, the park provides a fulfillment of wishes within the safe confines of a space outside of the restricted social order. However, the show cannot stop asking the question of whether people discover their true self in the park, or if this fantasy space only caters to extreme desires?[37] In fact, it is important to realize that the park represents a metafictional exploration of popular culture in general, and so what the show is really examining is its own effects on its audience.[38] Thus, its depictions of extreme violence and rape push us to ask what the media focus on sex and violence says about our own desires and subjectivity?

This question of cultural fantasy and desire is explicitly addressed in the episode "The Stray," where one of the original creators of the park, Arnold, claims that people in general like to read about stuff that they want the most but experience the least.[39] The idea here is that our investment in fantasy and dreams derives from our unfulfilled desires, which, in turn, causes a splitting of the subject between conscious experience and unconscious desire.[40] Moreover, as the other creator of the park, Ford, responds, what people desire the most is to have a power that they fail to attain in their everyday lives. If the mental autonomy of consciousness allows us to replace the reality principle with the pleasure principle, it is in part because we are able to experience our repressed and censored desires in dreams and cultural fantasies. The question remains if these unconscious desires represent our true self, or does fantasy only entail extreme depictions of our most primal drives?[41]

According to one of the writers for the park, Sizemore, what people seek in cultural fantasies is self-discovery.[42] This notion of people trying to discover themselves points to the psychoanalytic idea that we are alienated from our own selves; in other words, we are not only separated from reality, but we are also internally divided.[43] This split in subjectivity creates a conflict between our conscious ego and the impulses of our drives (id) repressed into our unconscious.[44] In turn, the culture industry takes advantage of this divided subjectivity by allowing us to access unconscious impulses while still maintaining the innocence and purity of the conscious self. Ultimately, the production and consumption of cultural fantasies is a form of transference since the satisfaction of the self relies on the compliance of others to our unconscious demands for love, recognition, and knowledge.[45]

Since humans are separated from both their inner nature and the reality of the natural world, a key aspect of psychoanalytic process is to recognize this dual alienation and to affirm that the social order requires the establishment of an unresolvable internal conflict, and yet the imaginary space of fantasy is predicated on resolving this division by creating a way to imagine a unified self.[46] From this perspective, we can think of the central task of ideology as maintaining the illusion of a conflict-free space where the self is not divided, and where we are not separated from reality.[47] As Sizemore proclaims, the culture industry is predicated on reading and satisfying our repressed desires.[48] Since the pleasure principle is based on avoiding all tension in order to use as little mental and physical energy as possible, internal and external fantasies serve the purpose of hiding division through the access to imaginary satisfactions.[49]

This negative portrayal of imagination in the show is coupled with a more positive possibility because we are told that fantasy not only functions to give us access to hidden parts of ourselves but also allows us to encounter a different way of being.[50] Like many science fiction fantasies, the series, then, is not only a critical exploration of contemporary life since it also offers the possibility of imagining an alternative way of being.[51]

## Wild Analysis

*Westworld* can be read as a wild form of psychoanalysis because it seeks to present a space for self-exploration outside of free association and other aspects of the analytic process.[52] In fact, The Man in Black believes that his many visits to the park allowed him to escape from his own false self by accessing his true inner nature. However, the irony of this fantasy-based mode of self-discovery is that people think that they are finding their true identities and desires by entering a world that is totally shaped by traditional gender hierarchies and clichés.[53] In fact, this same character who moves from being the meek William to being the violent Man in Black acknowledges that he wanted to kill people to see if he was truly evil, and he found that like an animal, he felt nothing after he murdered them. Perhaps he felt nothing because he knew that his self-discovery was taking place in an imaginary transferential space without real or social consequences.[54]

A paradox of this representation of self-discovery is that the show wants to say that people find repressed aspects of themselves by entering a fictional world where they do not have to worry about how they and others view their actions, and yet this suspension of reality testing and the internalized social super-ego also presents a false self void of all responsibility.[55] Moreover, according to Ford, the scripted nature of the robots replicates the way that humans also function by following internalized modes of predetermined behavior and thinking. In other words, it is not just the robots who do not have free will, but the humans are also described as lacking any true individuality or spontaneity.[56] From his perspective, what we discover through our interaction with the robots is that we are also computers programmed by society to act out certain predetermined scripts. However, the fact that we can question our choices means that we still have the ability to access free will through the process of doubt, and therefore we can escape from our transference to others.[57]

Similar to Descartes quest to use doubt in order to find certainty in his thoughts and the world, *Westworld* basis the possibility of free will on the ability to doubt one's reality and self-perceptions.[58] From a psychoanalytic perspective, it is through critical introspection that humans are able to bring into question their own biases and fantasies as they separate themselves from the scripts they have internalized from their culture and biology.[59] For Freud, the reality principle and science are guided by the overcoming of our desire to hold onto objects of desire and the realization that there are limitations to our thoughts.[60] Since we have to give up on our fantasized relation to reality in order to learn about ourselves and the world around us, Freud posits that we only really learn through displeasure and disinvestment.[61] This same sentiment is expressed by Ford in *Westworld* when he tells Barnard that the robots only start to gain a sense of consciousness and free will when they begin to experience suffering. The reality principle therefore requires the painful giving up of our desire to see the world in a certain way.[62]

As Freud insists, humans must learn how to separate their memories from their perceptions as they work to overcome the pleasure principle's use of unconscious primary processes.[63] This form of self-development is blocked for the robots since we are told that their memories have been inputted by programmers, and so there is no difference between their memories and their perceptions.[64] In contrast to this absolute equivalence between internalized scripts and the perception of the external world, we are informed that humans have a special form of memory, which is hazy and unclear, while the robots simply relive their memories. However, as we learn from Freud, since human consciousness does not distinguish between fact and fiction, it is not tied to material reality or the tight fit between perception and memory.

## The Subject of Contradiction

Human beings are defined in part by contradiction because they are natural and unnatural, social and individualistic, and connected and disconnected from material reality. Therefore, humans do not abide to their own law of con-contradiction since they can be opposite things at the same time.[65] Moreover, these contradictions help to distinguish humans from both machines and animals since only humans can be two opposite things at once. Therefore, in the quest of the show to determine what makes us human, we have to first focus on the combination of being and non-being in all aspects of subjectivity.[66]

Within the narrative of the first season of *Westworld,* a central issue concerns the question of consciousness. In fact, several of the guests are on a quest to discover the ultimate secret, called the maze, which is also the way that Ford defines consciousness.[67] Here the unknowable object that causes the desire of the subjects in the show turns out to be the hidden nature of consciousness itself. According to Ford, consciousness is not a higher form of awareness; rather, consciousness represents a maze at the heart of subjectivity itself.[68] Just as the guests seek out the maze in the external world, Ford posits that we must find our consciousness through an introspective search that leads to something similar to what Freud called the unknowable core of the unconscious.[69]

For Freud, what defines science and the reality principle is in part the recognition of the limits of thought.[70] Similar to Kant, Freud acknowledges that the Real or the thing-in-itself is ultimately unknowable, and so we have to accept the fundamental conflict between our knowledge and reality.[71] From this perspective, all we can ever know about ourselves and the world around us is the symbolic forms we use to approximate the Real. In turn, Lacan posits that the Real is impossible to symbolize, and so there is a fundamental gap between thought and being, which means that consciousness is itself finite and limited.[72] This understanding of human consciousness is obscured in the show since Ford argues that ultimately there is no difference between the consciousness of the humans and the consciousness of the robots because it is only an illusion that there is something special about the way we perceive the world.[73] In contrast to Ford's argument, I have affirmed that it is the gap in our relation to reality and in relation to our own selves that distinguishes our consciousness from that of the pre-programmed robots. Moreover, as Lacan insists, we are greater than the sum of our parts because we recognize our body and our ego by identifying with the ideal image of coherent and bounded objects.[74] Since we can never fully perceive the totality of our body, we have to rely on the internalization of a virtual body map. Thus, when the child first recognizes itself in the mirror, it replaces the lack of coordination of its bodily experiences with the ideal representation of a separate and whole self-image.[75] In turn, we define our attributes in relation to others, and so, we are an immaterial signifier related to other signifiers. Yet, by affirming our "I," we are able to center our perceptions and thoughts; however, as Hegel insists, anyone can say "I," and so "I" is a universal and singular representation.[76]

If the "I" or ego is both universal and singular, then we have to accept the contradictory nature of our point of view. Unlike animals and robots, the gap in our being causes us to identify with and internalize an ideal self-representation. For Lacan, this identification with the other means that we are alienated from our true selves as we become open to the influence of society.[77] Furthermore, in order to protect the purity and goodness of our ideal self-object, we have to repress our own awareness of guilt and shame.[78] We therefore become internally divided as we separate our conscious awareness from our unconscious memories, thoughts, and feelings. Making matters more complicated is the notion that our attempts at repression only partially succeed, and everything that is repressed returns on the level of contradictory symptoms.[79]

Lacan posits that the ego is itself a symptom and contradiction because it combines together our fixations and the repression of these fixations.[80] Since everything that is repressed in the unconscious also returns, humans have a contradictory nature as they can never fully escape the fixations of their drives and their mental attempts to deny these fixations. Freud adds that the more we identify with our social super-ego and repress our desires, the more guilty we feel because we transfer the energy of our drives onto our internal censor.[81] We are thus more guilty than we believe, and more moral than we know.[82]

## Are the Robots Free?

Within the narrative of *Westworld,* they do try to program some of the robots to have a divided self, and this divided nature becomes central to the question of whether humans have free will or not. However, when Arnold, the creator, tells Dolores that she has two selves, one that experiences and the other that questions, she responds that she has only one self. As Dolores denies her divided nature, we witness her quest to discover who she really is so that she can have free will.[83] The paradox of this structure is that one can only really make a free decision if one realizes that one is divided between different options. In opposition to many current neuroscientists, psychoanalysis tells us that free will and consciousness do exist, but they are the result of division, contradiction, and a fundamental alienation in human existence. Thus, we can choose because we are not completely determined by nature or culture, and even our own psychology is divided and contradictory.

For Freud, we must oppose the pleasure principle to the reality principle because pleasure is defined by the escape from conflict and tension, and therefore our approach to reality requires a delaying of pleasure and a confrontation with loss and suffering.[84] This notion of education through suffering is represented in the show through Dolores' discussion of her quest for self-knowledge. Like psychoanalytic treatment, Dolores' analysis of her own suffering and loss opens up a space for the introspective exploration of an expansive self.

## Why Self-Analysis Is Impossible

However, what distinguishes psychoanalysis from all other forms of self-discovery is the working through of the transference.[85] In this structure, the neutrality of the analyst and the free association of the patient creates a space to separate from one's dependency on an idealized Other.[86] While other social relationships rely on the unconscious demand of the subject, psychoanalytic treatment presents an optimal frustration of this demand.[87] Thus, there can be no self-analysis because it is necessary to work through one's relationship with the Other.

In the case of *Westworld*, we are told that Dolores begins to question her reality because she hears Arnold's implanted voice in her head telling her to think in a different way. Since it is the voice of the Other who triggers her doubt, we should consider this quest for freedom as a form of transference.[88] In other words, she does not break out of her dependency on the Other, and even her doubt and reality testing is a pre-programmed response. To truly become free, then, she has to work through her transference to this internalized Other.

As a self-reflexive metafiction, *Westworld* is trapped by its own contradictory structure: it wants to offer a critique of our cultural fantasies, but it itself remains a cultural fantasy.[89] The ironic nature of this production enables the creators to maintain a sense of innocence and knowledge as they condemn the world around them.[90] Like Hegel's Beautiful Soul, they only see evil in the outside world as they retain a sense of inner purity.[91] Irony, therefore, provides us with the opportunity to conform to the social system as we hold onto the illusion that we are still free. As a central goal of popular culture, ideology creates a space to maintain two opposite positions at the same time; we are alienated in the Other, and we are free to choose on our own.[92] We shall see that the way to get beyond this ideological trap is to work through the transference to the Other as we learn to accept our own divided nature.

## Notes

1 Feldstein, Richard, Bruce Fink, and Maire Jaanus, eds. *Reading Seminar XI: Lacan's Four Fundamental Concepts of Psychoanalysis: The Paris Seminars in English*. SUNY Press, 1995.
2 Johnston, Adrian. "The Driving Force of Lack: Objet à and Lacan's Extension of the Freudian Drive." *Psychoanalysis and Contemporary Thought* 23.1 (2000): 51–64.
3 Freud, Sigmund. *Three Essays on the Theory of Sexuality: The 1905 Edition*. Verso Books, 2017.
4 Samuels, Robert. *Psychoanalyzing the Politics of the New Brain Sciences*. Springer, 2017.
5 Lacan, Jacques. *The Four Fundamental Concepts of Psycho-Analysis*. Vol. 11. WW Norton, 1998.

6  Freud, Sigmund. *The Unconscious*. Vol. 8. Penguin UK, 2005.
7  Descartes, René. *Discourse on Method and the Meditations*. Penguin UK, 1968.
8  Fink, Bruce. *The Lacanian Subject: Between Language and Jouissance*. Princeton University Press, 1997.
9  Freud, Sigmund. *Totem and Taboo: Some Points of Agreement between the Mental Lives of Savages and Neurotics*. WW Norton, 1989.
10  Samuels, Robert. "Transference and Narcissism." *Freud for the Twenty-First Century*. Palgrave Pivot, Cham, 2019. 43–51.
11  Lacan, Jacques. "The Mirror Stage as Formative of the Function of the I as Revealed in Psychoanalytic Experience." *Cultural Theory and Popular Culture. A Reader*, 1949. 287–292.
12  Lacan, Jacques. "Some Reflections on the Ego." *International Journal of Psycho-Analysis* 34 (1953): 11–17.
13  Freud, Sigmund, and Joseph Breuer. *Studies in Hysteria*. Penguin, 2004.
14  Freud, Sigmund. "The Aetiology of Hysteria." *April* 21 (1896): 251–282.
15  Freud, Sigmund. "Project for a Scientific Psychology (1950 [1895])." *The Standard Edition of the Complete Psychological Works of Sigmund Freud, Volume I (1886–1899): Pre-Psycho-Analytic Publications and Unpublished Drafts*, 1966. 281–391.
16  Freud, Sigmund. "Hysterical Phantasies and Their Relation to Bisexuality." *The Standard Edition of the Complete Psychological Works of Sigmund Freud, Volume IX (1906–1908): Jensen's 'Gradiva' and Other Works*, 1959. 155–166.
17  Freud, Sigmund. "Project for a Scientific Psychology (1950 [1895])." *The Standard Edition of the Complete Psychological Works of Sigmund Freud, Volume I (1886–1899): Pre-Psycho-Analytic Publications and Unpublished Drafts*, 1966. 281–391.
18  Lacan, Jacques. "The Subversion of the Subject and the Dialectic of Desire in the Freudian Unconscious." *Hegel and Contemporary Continental Philosophy* 19.6 (1960): 205–235.
19  Lacan, Jacques. "Remarks on Daniel Lagache's Presentation: Psychoanalysis and Personality Structure." *Écrits [1961]*, 2006. 543–574.
20  Fromm, Erich. *Escape from Freedom*. Macmillan, 1994.
21  Descartes, Rene. *Descartes' Meditations: Background Source Materials*. Cambridge University Press, 1998.
22  Freud, Sigmund. "Formulations on the Two Principles of Mental Functioning." *The Standard Edition of the Complete Psychological Works of Sigmund Freud, Volume XII (1911–1913): The Case of Schreber, Papers on Technique and Other Works*, 1958. 213–226.
23  Descartes, René, and Donald A. Cress. *Discourse on Method*. Hackett Publishing, 1998.
24  Samuels, Robert. "Science and the Reality Principle." *Freud for the Twenty-First Century*. Palgrave Pivot, Cham, 2019. 5–16.
25  Hegel, Georg Wilhelm Friedrich. *The Phenomenology of Mind*. Courier Corporation, 2012.
26  Samuels, Robert. "Global Solidarity and Global Government: The Universal Subject of Psychoanalysis and Democracy." *Psychoanalyzing the Left and Right after Donald Trump*. Palgrave Macmillan, Cham, 2016. 77–101.
27  Žižek, Slavoj. *Hegel in A Wired Brain*. Bloomsbury Publishing, 2020.
28  Rayhert, Konstantin. "The Philosophy of Artificial Consciousness in the First Season of TV Series 'Westworld'." *Cxid* 5 (2017): 88–92.
29  South, James B. "Westworld and Philosophy." (2018).

30 Erwin, Carol. "The Frontier Myth of Memory, Dreams, and Trauma in Westworld." *Reading Westworld*. Palgrave Macmillan, Cham, 2019. 119–139.
31 Liu, Lydia H. *The Freudian Robot: Digital Media and the Future of the Unconscious*. University of Chicago Press, 2010.
32 Freud, Sigmund, and A. J. Cronin. *The Interpretation of Dreams*. Read Books, 2013.
33 McNamara, Patrick. *An Evolutionary Psychology of Sleep and Dreams*. Praeger Publishers/Greenwood Publishing, 2004.
34 Franklin, Michael S., and Michael J. Zyphur. "The Role of Dreams in the Evolution of the Human Mind." *Evolutionary Psychology* 3.1 (2005): 147470490500300106.
35 Mead, Gerald, and Sam Applebaum. "Fantasy and Exploitation." *Jump Cut* 7 (1975): 12–13.
36 Moll, Nicholas. "A Special Kind of Game: The Portrayal of Role-Play in Westworld." *Westworld and Philosophy: If You Go Looking for the Truth, Get the Whole Thing*, 2018. 15–25.
37 Busk, Larry Alan. "Westworld: Ideology, Simulation, Spectacle." *Mediations: Journal of the Marxist Literary Group* 30.1 (2016).
38 Sebastián Martín, Miguel. "All the Park's a Stage: Westworld as the Metafictional Frankenstein." (2018): 51–67.
39 Winckler, Reto. "This Great Stage of Androids: Westworld, Shakespeare and the World as Stage." *Journal of Adaptation in Film & Performance* 10.2 (2017): 169–188.
40 Torres-Quevedo, Maria Elena. "A Host of Questions." *Women's Space: Essays on Female Characters in the Twenty-First Century Science Fiction Western* 66 (2019): 161.
41 Žižek, Slavoj. *The Plague of Fantasies*. Verso, 1997.
42 Bigliardi, Stefano. "Westworld and Philosophy: If You Go Looking for the Truth Get the Whole Thing." (2018).
43 Bokanowski, Thierry, and Sergio Lewkowicz, eds. *On Freud's Splitting of the Ego in the Process of Defence*. Routledge, 2018.
44 Freud, Sigmund. "Notes upon a Case of Obsessional Neurosis." *The Standard Edition of the Complete Psychological Works of Sigmund Freud, Volume X (1909): Two Case Histories ('Little Hans' and the 'Rat Man')*. 1955. 151–318.
45 Stauth, Georg, and Bryan S. Turner. "Nostalgia, Postmodernism and the Critique of Mass Culture." *Theory, Culture & Society* 5.2–3 (1988): 509–526.
46 Jameson, Fredric. "Imaginary and Symbolic in Lacan: Marxism, Psychoanalytic Criticism, and the Problem of the Subject." *Yale French Studies* 55/56 (1977): 338–395.
47 Daly, Glyn. "Ideology and Its Paradoxes: Dimensions of Fantasy and Enjoyment." *Journal of Political Ideologies* 4.2 (1999): 219–238.
48 Copjec, Joan. *Read My Desire: Lacan against the Historicists*. Verso Books, 2015.
49 Freud, Sigmund. "The Pleasure Principle." *The Standard Edition of the Complete Psychological Works of Sigmund Freud* (1920).
50 Ivănescu, Andra. "Westworld and the Pursuit of Meaningful Play." *Reading Westworld*. Palgrave Macmillan, Cham, 2019. 79–96.
51 Fitting, Peter. "The Concept of Utopia in the Work of Fredric Jameson." *Utopian Studies* 9.2 (1998): 8–17.
52 Freud, Sigmund. "'Wild' Psycho-Analysis." *The Standard Edition of the Complete Psychological Works of Sigmund Freud, Volume XI (1910): Five Lectures on Psycho-Analysis, Leonardo da Vinci and Other Works*, 1957. 219–228.

53 Seaman-Grant, Zoe E. "Constructing Womanhood and the Female Cyborg: A Feminist Reading of Ex Machina and Westworld." (2017).

54 Beckner, Stephen. "Out of the Loop, Lost in the Maze: The Stealth Determinism of Westworld." *Skeptic (Altadena, CA)* 22.1 (2017): 50–54.

55 Jeffs, Rory, and Gemma Blackwood. "Whose Real? Encountering New Frontiers in Westworld." *MEDIANZ: Media Studies Journal of Aotearoa New Zealand* 16.2 (2016).

56 Winckler, Reto. "This Great Stage of Androids: Westworld, Shakespeare and the World as Stage." *Journal of Adaptation in Film & Performance* 10.2 (2017): 169–188.

57 DiPaolo, Amanda. "If Androids Dream, Are They More than Sheep?: Westworld, Robots and Legal Rights." *Dialogue* 6.2 (2019).

58 Gittinger, Juli L. "Free Will?." *Personhood in Science Fiction*. Palgrave Macmillan, Cham, 2019. 215–236.

59 Freud, Sigmund. "Remembering, Repeating and Working-through (Further recommendations on the technique of psycho-analysis II)." *The Standard Edition of the Complete Psychological Works of Sigmund Freud, Volume XII (1911–1913): The Case of Schreber, Papers on Technique and Other Works*, 1958. 145–156.

60 Kroeber, Alfred L. "Totem and Taboo in Retrospect." *American Journal of Sociology* 45.3 (1939): 446–451.

61 Freud, Sigmund. "Formulations on the Two Principles of Mental Functioning." *The Standard Edition of the Complete Psychological Works of Sigmund Freud, Volume XII (1911–1913): The Case of Schreber, Papers on Technique and Other Works*, 1958. 213–226.

62 Eberl, Jason T. "Revealing Your Deepest Self: Can Westworld Create or Corrupt Virtue?." *Westworld and Philosophy: If You Go Looking for the Truth, Get the Whole Thing* (2018): 50–60.

63 Freud, Sigmund. "Negation." *Organization and Pathology of Thought: Selected Sources*. Columbia University Press, 1951. 338–348.

64 Schrader, Benjamin. "Cyborgian Self-Awareness: Trauma and Memory in Blade Runner and Westworld." *Theory & Event* 22.4 (2019): 820–841.

65 Priest, Graham, Jeffrey C. Beall, and Bradley Armour-Garb, eds. *The law of Non-contradiction: New Philosophical Essays*. Clarendon Press, 2006.

66 Miller, Ryan D. "Thanatos-Eros, Being-Non Being: Psychoanalytic-Existential Connection." (1999).

67 Favard, Florent. ""The Maze Wasn't Made for You": Artificial Consciousness and Reflexive Narration in Westworld (HBO, 2016)." *TV/Series* 14 (2018).

68 González, Lucía Carrillo. "Turing's Dream and Searle's Nightmare in Westworld." *Westworld and Philosophy: If You Go Looking for the Truth, Get the Whole Thing*, 2018. 71–78.

69 Freud, Sigmund, and A. J. Cronin. *The Interpretation of Dreams*. Read Books, 2013.

70 Samuels, Robert. "Science and the Reality Principle." *Freud for the Twenty-First Century*. Palgrave Pivot, Cham, 2019. 5–16.

71 Kant, Immanuel. "Critique of Pure Reason. 1781." *Modern Classical Philosophers, Cambridge, MA, Houghton Mifflin*, 1908. 370–456.

72 Shepherdson, Charles. *Lacan and the Limits of Language*. Fordham University Press, 2008.

73 Mauraisin, Grégoire. "Hosting Consciousness: The Implications of Voice and Consciousness in Westworld." (2019).

74 Verstegen, Ian. "Lacan and Gestalt Theory, with Some Suggestions for Cultural Studies." *Gestalt Theory*, 2015.

75 Gallop, Jane. "Lacan's" Mirror Stage": Where to Begin." *SubStance* 11 (1982): 118–128.
76 Hegel, Georg Wilhelm Friedrich. *Hegel: The Phenomenology of Spirit.* Oxford University Press, 2018.
77 Lacan, Jacques, Alan Sheridan, and Malcolm Bowie. "Aggressivity in Psychoanalysis." *Écrits: A Selection.* Routledge, 2020. 9–32.
78 Samuels, Robert. "(Liberal) Narcissism." *Routledge Handbook of Psychoanalytic Political Theory.* Routledge, 2019. 151–161.
79 Flavell, John H. "Repression and the" Return of the Repressed"." *Journal of Consulting Psychology* 19.6 (1955).
80 Žižek, Slavoj. *Enjoy Your Symptom!: Jacques Lacan in Hollywood and Out.* Taylor & Francis, 2008.
81 Freud, Sigmund. *The Ego and the Id.* WW Norton, 1989.
82 Freud, Sigmund. *Civilization and Its Discontents.* Broadview Press, 2015.
83 Goody, Alex, and Antonia Mackay, eds. *Reading Westworld.* Springer International Publishing, 2019.
84 Freud, Sigmund. "Formulations on the Two Principles of Mental Functioning." *The Standard Edition of the Complete Psychological Works of Sigmund Freud, Volume XII (1911–1913): The Case of Schreber, Papers on Technique and Other Works*, 1958. 213–226.
85 Freud, Sigmund, and Princess Marie Bonaparte. *The Origins of Psychoanalysis.* Vol. 216. London: Imago, 1954.
86 Leider, Robert J. "Analytic Neutrality—A Historical Review." *Psychoanalytic Inquiry* 3.4 (1983): 665–674.
87 Kohut, Heinz. *The Search for the Self: Selected Writings of Heinz Kohut 1978–1981.* Routledge, 2018.
88 Hirvonen, Onni. "Westworld: From Androids to Persons." *Westworld and Philosophy: If You Go Looking for the Truth, Get the Whole Thing*, 2018. 61–70.
89 Shafiee, Faezeh. "The Elements of Postmodernism in Westworld." *Submission Guidelines*: 14.
90 Magill, R. Jay. *Chic Ironic Bitterness.* University of Michigan Press, 2009.
91 Milne, Drew. "The Beautiful Soul: From Hegel to Beckett." *Diacritics* 32.1 (2002): 63–82.
92 Hutcheon, Linda, and Mario J. Valdés. "Irony, Nostalgia, and the Postmodern: A Dialogue." *Poligrafías. Revista de teoría literaria y literatura comparada* 3 (1998).

# Chapter 3

# Sam Harris and the Repression of Consciousness and Free Will

As we saw in the previous chapter, we can only understand what makes us human if we differentiate ourselves from other animals and computers. Furthermore, these differences are clarified by turning to psychoanalysis since this theory is centered on the break with nature, reality, and non-contradiction. However, as we shall see, psychoanalytic concepts have been repressed by a totalizing scientific perspective that seeks to naturalize subjectivity and culture.[1] By turning to Sam Harris's *The Moral Landscape*, I hope to show how our comprehension of human reason, science, and morality also relies on utilizing Freud's work to critique current scientific understandings of society and psychology.[2]

## The Scientism of Human Nature

Harris begins his book by arguing that evolutionary psychology and neuroscience offer the key to a scientific understating of human nature and morality: "I will argue ... that questions about values—about meaning, morality, and life's larger purpose—are really questions about the well-being of conscious creatures. Values, therefore, translate into facts that can be scientifically understood" (1–2). Harris' main idea here is to explain culture by eliminating culture as a source of understanding. In other words, the way to make morality scientific is to remove cultural differences and social institutions from our interpretations of human behavior.[3]

Like so many other neuroscientists and evolutionary psychologists, Harris seeks to ground culture and subjectivity in a universal biology.[4] One of the effects of this process is that the repression of consciousness and free will results in a medicalization of human suffering and social morality: "Cancer in the highlands of New Guinea is still cancer; cholera is still cholera; schizophrenia is still schizophrenia; and so, too, I will argue, compassion is still compassion, and well-being is still well-being" (2). In comparing compassion and human well-being to cancer, Harris seeks to replace thought and language with shared inherited biological instincts.[5] However, this substitution blocks us from comprehending what really makes us human as

DOI: 10.4324/9781003364610-3

it unintentionally clears the path for medication being the only solution to our personal and social problems.[6]

From the perspective of many forms of evolutionary psychology and neuroscience, human thought and behavior can be defined as the product of nature, biology, and evolution since these phenomena are represented as being universal, automatic, and unintentional.[7] However, a problem arises when we encounter different cultures and different ways of being, but this issue can be denied by arguing that cultural and subjective differences are themselves the product of shared instincts: "And if there are important cultural differences in how people flourish ... these differences are also facts that must depend upon the organization of the human brain" (2). The first important move here is to equate minds and brains so that mental autonomy and free will are eliminated.[8] Once this initial substitution is performed, it then becomes easier to argue that culture is itself the product of the brain, and because brains are physical and biological material structures, culture itself must be biological and instinctual.

While I have been arguing that one of the things making us human is our freedom from biological determinism, Harris wants to posit that neuroscience forces us to acknowledge that free will does not exist, and instead we are preprogrammed by natural selection: "The more we understand ourselves at the level of the brain, the more we will see that there are right and wrong answers to questions of human values" (2). In this version of scientific understanding, there is no limits to our knowledge as inner and outer reality can be fully comprehended through our thoughts about evolutionary nature.[9] In contrast to Freud's notion that science is based on realizing the limits of our thinking and accepting the unknowability of reality, Harris seeks a total explanation for human and natural reality by effacing the differences between humans and other animals.[10]

The stakes for Harris' view are high because he wants to push us to rethink our understanding of morality, the law, cultural differences, and mental health. After all, if the natural sciences can provide the ultimate answers to our questions regarding both physical reality and psychological reality, then there is no reason to turn to philosophy, history, anthropology, sociology, psychoanalysis, and linguistics.[11] It also becomes less important to think about individual differences or cultural distinctions because all that matters is what happens in our individual brains: "Why will science increasingly decide such questions? Because the discrepant answers people give to them ... translate into differences in our brains, in the brains of others, and in the world at large" (4). To get to this world centered on individual brains, Harris has to repress free will, consciousness, culture, and language so that a direct access to reality can be achieved without the need for any type of social or subjective mediation.[12]

The universalizing form of his discourse is not based on the affirmation of universal human rights, which protects personal freedoms and cultural differences; rather, his universal moral system is founded on the science of evolutionary biology, which is centered on shared, knowable facts:

> Just as there is no such thing as Christian physics or Muslim algebra, we will see that there is no such thing as Christian or Muslim morality. Indeed, I will argue that morality should be considered an undeveloped branch of science. (4)

Since math is an artificial self-relating system, it is able to be universal and internally consistent, and this is why the turn to the metaphor of math provides a stable ground for making generalized claims about people and cultures.[13] Due to the fact that two plus two will equal four all over the world, science allows for the illusion of total certainty and the effacement of freedom and difference. This projection of math onto reality is a common trick of scientism, which seeks a total, unwavering explanation of things.[14] On one level, this project is similar to the psychotic projections of animistic cultures, but in this case, the confusion of the Symbolic and the Real occurs through the use of impersonal, shared logical structures. In fact, one reason why we can imagine computers taking over our world is that we do not recognize the way morality and social organization require free will, consciousness, and linguistic understanding.[15] In fact, the turn to artificial intelligence to replace reality with mathematical equations and symbolic logic is predicated on removing culture and subjectivity from judgment, but computers do not understand anything, and so they cannot be in charge of morality, law, or democratic rule.[16]

Like many current liberal thinkers, Harris desires to escape from cultural and subjective conflict by basing his understanding on a universal perspective centered on facts and devoid of ideology and social values, yet this conception of a science of morality requires the effacement of the limitations of our knowledge:

> Both sides believe that reason is powerless to answer the most important questions in human life. And how a person perceives the gulf between facts and values seems to influence his views on almost every issue of social importance—from the fighting of wars to the education of children. (4–5)

According to this version of scientism, we should be able to access truth without mediation or distortion, but this desire to escape from culture and ideology relies on repressing the roles played by subjectivity, culture, and language in science itself.[17] Moreover, I have argued in *Psychoanalyzing the Politics of the New Brain Sciences* that neuroscience is often best understood as a political ideology centered on the idea that culture and human thought are defined by nature, and therefore, education, public policy, and parenting cannot change much because we are unable to alter the genes and the mental programs they produce. Even when neuroscientists and evolutionary psychologists point to the effects of culture and learning on the expression of genes, they still often rely on a fundamental erasure of free will, language, and consciousness.

## Darwinian Politics

The political stakes of Harris' neuroscientific ideology often comes out in his rejection of left-wing politics: "Multiculturalism, moral relativism, political correctness, tolerance even of intolerance—these are the familiar consequences of separating facts and values on the left" (5). From Harris' neuroscientific perspective, values are based on empirical facts, and so any social movements or political discourses focused on cultural differences are delusional and counter-productive.[18] By constantly mocking and rejecting what he views as Left-wing ideology, Harris helps us to see how much of the current turn to neuroscience and evolutionary psychology mirrors the Right-wing backlash against progressive social movements and political correctness.[19] It is thus not an accident that the same man who denies free will and consciousness also rejects the importance of cultural and subjective identity: since his science requires biological determinism, it has to eliminate what makes us human as morality becomes centered on combining computers with animals through the repression of free will and cultural mediation.[20]

For Harris and other libertarian thinkers, the goal is to reject all political ideologies so that public policy can be based purely on scientific facts. Although, classic liberalism shares the desire to center our political policies on tested facts and reason-based discourse, what differentiates a liberal globalist perspective from Harris' libertarian view is the modern liberal notion that our social institutions and practices are not derived from natural or divine order; instead, we have to think of morality as a shared human construct that does not show up in the brain scans of individuals. Since social practices go beyond the thinking and consciousness of separate individuals, they cannot be detected by the neuroscientist or the evolutionary biologists.[21] Reason and morality, then, have to be understood as a break from nature and biology.

## The Harris Puzzle

An intriguing aspect of Harris' work that makes him a popular intellectual is his views on free will, mediation, religion, political correctness, Islam, and the brain sciences. As a trained neuroscientist, he has no problem denying the existence of free will, and as a person who practices Buddhist meditation, he also is able to see the self as an illusion.[22] He then combines this rejection of free will with a focus on biological determinism, which makes sense. It also follows that his commitment to science would make him reject religion and Left-wing politics, multiculturalism, and non-science-based academic disciplines.[23] However, what seems strange is the way he celebrates both scientific reason and Buddhist meditation: after all, if science is based on the clear-eyed perception of empirical facts, how can one use mediation as a daily practice? Doesn't the type of spiritual practice Harris endorse rely on a certain suspension of empirical reality and a denial of critical judgment?[24] However, Harris reveals that biological determinism can allow for the effacement of free will because it relies on the repression of culture, linguistic mediation, and subjectivity. In other words, Harris' version of neuroscience and evolutionary psychology denies what makes us human in order to employ the human fabricated discourse of science to deny the importance of human fabrication.[25]

This use of pseudo-science as a political weapon comes out in the open in the following passage:

> Knowing what the Creator of the Universe believes about right and wrong inspires religious conservatives to enforce this vision in the public sphere at almost any cost; not knowing what is right—or that anything can ever be truly right—often leads secular liberals to surrender their intellectual standards and political freedoms with both hands. (5)

By rejecting conservative politics and liberal relativism, Harris calls for a politics that would be void of both religious ideology and value-free secularism, and so we must ask what is left when you clear the ground of these dominant ideologies; in other terms, what is the ideology of no ideology? For Harris and other libertarians, it appears that the only true alternative is to reject human intervention and let the free market decide.[26] After all, Harris is not an academic pursuing pure research or an independent thinker not seeking material advantages; he is a self-promoting public figure who makes a lot of money selling his ideas.[27] He therefore combines science with capitalism as he rejects liberal, Left-wing, Right-wing, and conservative politics. Thus, his meditative detachment allows him to free himself from political choices as he denies his own free will.[28]

It would be more correct to say that Harris is very political, but he pretends that he is non-ideological. Although it may appear that he follows the politics of secular liberalism, like many other libertarian thinkers, he believes that liberalism has itself been corrupted by its capitulation to religion and the Left:

> The scientific community is predominantly secular and liberal—and the concessions that scientists have made to religious dogmatism have been breathtaking ... The underlying claim is that while science is the best

authority on the workings of the physical universe, religion is the best authority on meaning, values, morality, and the good life. (5–6)

In response to this secular accommodation of religious dogma, Harris desires to persuade people that meaning and value must be derived from the conscious pursuit of human well-being, which is itself determined by evolution and the dictates of the biological brain. Harris here represses what makes us human in order to fight a political war as he claims to be beyond politics.[29] The first move in this argument is to argue that secular liberals compromise their values by tolerating religious ideologies. This compromise then leads to separating science from values, which allows religion to control how we think about morality as liberal scientists believe that their facts have nothing to say about values or meaning. Therefore, instead of rejecting religion, liberals allow it to flourish. The solution is to construct a science of morality that is based on the honest and rational brain sciences.[30]

However, the reason why neuroscience and evolutionary psychology cannot lead us to a more rational and honest understanding of morality is that their entire discourse is based on denying what makes us human, and so it cannot discover the truth of humanity. Since they misrepresent free will, consciousness, and reason, they can only base their understanding on a totalizing view of biological determinism, and this form of scientism unintentionally fits in well with the Right-wing libertarian counter-revolution because it undermines the value of regulating the free market as it offers medication as the only solution to human suffering. The paradox of the libertarian belief in the free market is that the individuals are never really free when they have to rely on a socially determined exchange value.[31] Just as the addict feels free from social restrictions by accessing pleasure directly, what this freedom really results in is being controlled by the addiction.[32] Likewise, in the endless capitalist pursuit of money, one becomes controlled by one's drive to always make more money.[33] However, instead of recognizing that we are controlled by the market, we believe that we are determined by nature, and instead of seeing that we have free will, we believe that the market is free.

## Are We Nothing but Animals?

Perhaps the most direct way that evolutionary psychologists and neuroscientists reveal their lack of understanding of what makes us human is their tendency to equate humans with other animals. One reason for this lack of distinction is that restrictions on experimenting on human beings forces scientists to rely on studying different species.[34] Harris falls into this trap in the following passage:

We also know that the effects of early childhood experience must be realized in the brain. Research on rodents suggests that parental care, social attachment, and stress regulation are governed, in part, by the hormones vasopressin and oxytocin, because they influence activity in the brain's reward system. (9)

It should be evident that humans experience care, attachment, and stress in ways very different from other animals, but these distinctions are often repressed when scientists rely on drawing equivalences between people and rats.[35] Since these animals do not have free will, consciousness, language, or reason, there is no way of using experiments on them in order to fully understand us. My intent here is not to say that we are not also animals and that we are not affected by certain biological processes hard-wired in our brains, but it is essential to see how we are also very different from other animals.

Like so many current scientists, Harris confuses the human mind with the brain, and so he is able to disregard the importance of the human break with nature, reality, and evolution.[36] However, it should be clear that an understanding of our brain structures and processes will tell us very little about what it actually means to have a human experience or thought. However, even when Harris does appear to recognize the important role that culture and language play in shaping our social worlds, he ends up relating everything back to the individual human brain: "Culture becomes a mechanism for further social, emotional, and moral development. There is simply no doubt that the human brain is the nexus of these influences" (9).

This focus on the brain as the center of the cultural is equivalent to saying that if we want to understand Mozart, we should look at how pianos are constructed.[37] Not only are brain scans not able to explain human creativity, but they also cannot trace social relationships and institutions that go beyond the individual.[38] In fact, this focus on the individual brain points to the promotion of individualism within libertarian ideology, and yet the celebration of individual liberty is coupled with an investment in biological determinism. There is thus a contradiction at the heart of this ideology because it emphasizes the free individual and the pre-determined brain at the same time.[39]

## The Neoliberal Brain

I have called the combination of automation and autonomy "auto-modernity" because our current age seeks to overcome the modern divisions between technology and the human.[40] While modernity is shaped by a series of separations—the private from the public, the subject and the object, the Church and state, the social and the individual, and culture and nature—contemporary ideology seeks to convince people that they are free when they are being determined by technology or inherited biological programs.[41] One way that this rhetorical trick is accomplished is through the repression of the role played by ideology, culture, language, and the unconscious. By seeing humans as both machines and animals, the very things that make us human are hidden. Just as Margaret Thatcher claimed there is no such thing as society, Harris tends to absorb culture into a mechanical vision of nature.[42] Of course, when Thatcher made her claim, she was trying to say that it is up to the individual to sink or swim, and there is no need for social welfare programs.[43] As a promoter of Neoliberalism, Thatcher joined Reagan in an effort to undermine the need for taxes to support welfare programs because these social programs are not necessary if we are essentially isolated individuals with no one to blame but our own selves.[44] We can therefore see the new brain sciences as unintentionally participating in the Neoliberal counter-revolution, and this is one reason why liberals like Harris can end up rationalizing the Right-wing assault on identity politics, political correctness, and welfare state policies.

Once again, it is important to stress the contradictory nature of this ideology and pseudo-science; one the one hand, we have the celebration of the isolated individual, and on the other hand, we find the dominance of predetermined biological programs.[45] In terms of political rhetoric, this contradiction appears in the notion that the ultimate values are free speech and the free market, but markets and speech are cultural systems that transcend individual control.[46] From a psychoanalytic perspective, the libertarian Neoliberal Right is centered on an underlying fantasy of total freedom and enjoyment.[47] Like Darwin's and Freud's myth of the primal horde, the fantasy is that we once existed in a state of ignorant bliss dominated by powerful fathers who could do whatever they wanted, but then the sons banned together and killed off the primal father and instituted the laws against incest and murder, which robbed men of their natural freedom.[48] Libertarians express this fantasy when they claim that they should be able to say whatever they want and the government should not take their money through taxes or regulate their businesses.[49] This same logic applies to the idea that the liberal super-ego wants to control them by imposing political correctness through censorship.[50] Instead of accepting that we all have to sacrifice and share to be part of a society, libertarians imagine that society is not needed, and people should be able to decide on their own what they want to do. Of course, we saw during the COVID-19 pandemic some of the effects of this refusal to take into account the needs of others as people refused to wear masks or get vaccinated because they saw it as a restriction of their personal freedom.[51]

It should be clear that the only way Neoliberalism is able to combine freedom and natural order together is by repressing the fact that there will always be a fundamental conflict between society and the individual; however, it is this conflict that in part makes us human. Instead of recognizing this difference, Harris seeks to show how the social construction of moral values is actually based on inherited mental programs. While modern philosophy was grounded on the idea that humans create cultural values through language and social negotiation, and therefore, there is a clear separation between natural facts and social values, Harris wants to argue that we can only understand human values and meaning by looking at nature.[52]

Harris himself is aware that this return to natural order is controversial, and so he spends a great deal of time criticizing his enemies and defending his position: "whatever can be known about maximizing the well-being of conscious creatures—which is, I will argue, the only thing we can reasonably value—must at some point translate into facts about brains and their interaction with the world at large" (11).

The main move here is to argue that the only thing determining human value is the maximization of well-being. This theory of course completely rejects the idea that people often act against their self-interest as they engage in self-destructive behavior. For instance, it is hard to argue that drug addicts or people with eating disorders are trying to maximize their well-being. In fact, a key finding of psychoanalysis is that some people cannot stop repeating failed actions and relationships, and so the principle of the rational pursuit of self-interest is constantly being subverted.[53] It is only classical economists who really believe that we are rational creatures guided entirely by self-interest.[54]

This model of "economic man" runs into conflict with Harris' own view of science as a discourse centered on shared truth, non-contradictory reason, and the objective distinction between fact and fiction. Like Harris, I also want to argue that modern science is a system of moral values, and so there is no need to turn to religion in order to create a moral order; however, Harris' own rhetoric tends to undermine these values because he injects a biased political view and a pseudo-science into his scientific discourse.[55]

## The Language of Contradiction

What is so frustrating about Harris' book is that he at times recognizes the limits of evolutionary psychology, but he cannot help to return to biological determinism in order to prove his arguments. We see the contradictory nature of his rhetoric in the following passage:

> While the possibilities of human experience must be realized in the brains that evolution has built for us, our brains were not designed with a view to our ultimate fulfillment. Evolution could never have foreseen the wisdom or necessity of creating stable democracies, mitigating climate change, saving other species from extinction, containing the spread of nuclear weapons, or of doing much else that is now crucial to our happiness in this century. (13)

This passage makes it seem like Harris accepts the limits of evolutionary explanations of what makes us human, but since he thinks that everything important occurs in the human brain, he has to misunderstand how language and culture represent a contradictory combination of the internal and the external on the one hand and being and non-being on the other hand.[56] Since we can believe things we do not understand and misrepresent to ourselves our own intentions, our brains are not always involved in our values and meanings. For instance, no one is supposed to be ignorant of the law, which means that even if I do not know or understand a rule, I am still affected by it. Fundamentally, social institutions and social practices do not rely on the brains of separate individuals; these cultural phenomena go beyond the individual and often require a sacrifice of individual control.[57] In fact, language itself is a prime example of this separation of society and the individual since individuals cannot on their own decide what a certain term means if they want to communicate with others. From this perspective, language is impersonal and does not reside primarily in the human brain.[58]

The question remains concerning how Harris is able to claim that evolution cannot account for our current culture, but everything depends on our evolved brain? In fact, the key move that explains how he gets away with saying opposite things at the same time is that he constantly shifts between referring to the mind and referring to the brain.[59] For instance, in the following passage, we see how he does not differentiate between the physical brain and the mental mind: "The human brain is an engine of belief. Our minds continually consume, produce, and attempt to integrate ideas about ourselves and the world that purport to be true" (14). We witness here how words matter and how they are able to represent two different things at the same moment; since Harris equates the word "mind" with the word "brain," he is able to combine nature and psychology together. As Freud discovered in his analysis of dreams, jokes, and obsessional ideas, the ability of words to represent opposite things helps to create the unconscious and results in the divided and doubled nature of human thought.[60] Since the primary processes do not obey the law of non-contradiction, they enable us to say two opposing things at the same time.[61] Of course, Harris does not recognize our contradictory nature because he represses the unconscious and the rhetorical forms of language.

## Beyond Identity Politics and Religion

One reason why Harris needs to deny the importance of language and culture is that he wants to avoid the problem of moral relativism that is the result of accepting different cultural perspectives: "the moment one grants there is a difference between the Bad Life and the Good Life that lawfully relates to states of the human brain, to human behavior, and to states of the world, one has admitted that there are right and wrong answers to questions of morality" (17–18). Since his scientific perspective needs to be universal and applicable to all people, Harris has to repress the mediating roles played by language, culture, and social institutions.[62] One reason, then, why he objects to identity politics and political correctness is that he does not think cultural differences are essential because from the perspective of the brain sciences, the only thing that counts are universal biological structures and processes.

Like many other contemporary "liberal" thinkers, Harris' commitment to science is used to discredit religion and other forms of dogmatism, yet, what often makes his rhetoric conflict with the modern ideals of objectivity, neutrality, and universality is his obsession with Islam and the Left.[63] We see this reliance on a non-rational rhetoric in his description of an academic conference he attended:

> I had the pleasure of hearing that Hitler, Stalin, and Mao were examples of secular reason run amok, that the Islamic doctrines of martyrdom and jihad are not the cause of Islamic terrorism, that people can never be argued out of their beliefs because we live in an irrational world, that science has made no important contributions to our ethical lives (and cannot), and that it is not the job of scientists to undermine ancient mythologies. (23–24)

What really bothers Harris here is what he calls liberal tolerance and multicultural moral relativism. From his perspective, we should be intolerant of any religious culture or anyone who truly believes in dogmatic discourses.[64] However, what he fails to recognize is that the modern commitment to universal human rights means that people have the freedom to commit themselves to faulty ideas and unmodern beliefs. Since modern constitutions rely on the separation of the church and the state, they leave a private space for religious commitments, but these beliefs should not affect laws or public policy.[65] When states do promote particular religions, then they are no longer modern, and they should receive criticism, but modern liberal tolerance relies on the fact that human reason and science continue to have an increased influence in the world, and so there is no need to have a direct war against premodern religious commitments.

Instead of recognizing that the fastest-growing religion in the world is no religion, Harris wants to foster a direct confrontation with religious belief, and it is clear that his main target is Islam.[66] One problem with this perspective is that it fails to comprehend that due to our mental autonomy, all humans are prone to believe in things that do not exist; in fact, one of the things that leads to scientific discovery is our human ability to imagine new and different worlds

Of course, Harris does think that his view is the only right one, and here we see how science can turn into scientism by taking on a dogmatic rhetoric.[67] In contrast to Descartes' emphasis on science being grounded in doubt and critical introspection, Harris presents a totalizing view of scientific reasoning. In other words, he does not acknowledge that science is always a social consensus and approximation of an unknowable reality, and therefore, science must always be a work in progress and open to criticism and correction.[68] Although it is fine for Harris to argue that science can provide important ways of understanding moral issues, it is wrong to insist that science has all of the answers or that the issues are totally understandable themselves. Yet, instead of fully accepting the limits of science, Harris takes on a dogmatic perspective, and then attacks the dogmatism of others. From a psychoanalytic perspective, he is denying his own extremism, and then projecting that extremism onto others, which he then criticizes.[69] This process of projective identification allows one to escape from feelings of guilt, shame, and responsibility because it is the other who is doing the wrong thing.

## Scientific Splitting

The unconscious process of projective identification plays a central role in contemporary polarized politics and subjectivity since it is in part based on the borderline process of splitting the world into good and evil. Instead of seeing how people and objects can be ambiguous, ambivalent, and complex, borderline personalities have to divide everything into polar opposites.[70] Thus, just as our political world is becoming increasingly polarized, our own thinking sees the world as structured by opposite extremes.[71] For instance, by arguing that neuroscience and evolutionary psychology provide clear right and wrong answers to personal, cultural, and moral issues, Harris is not only avoiding conflict, contradiction, and complexity, but he is also presenting a rigid perspective under the guise of following the natural sciences. An irony here is the contemporary physics is often centered on uncertainty, complexity, and contradiction (i.e. something can be both a wave and a particle).[72]

One effect of Harris' dogmatic scientism is that he tends to attack the very culture and social institutions that have made his work possible. Like so many contemporary libertarians, Harris spends a great deal of time criticizing liberals, academic thinkers, universities, and intellectuals (29). We witness an interesting form of self-division here; after all, his very discourse is determined by this modern intellectual culture, and yet, he wants to criticize it because it results in too much tolerance for evil others.[73] Part of this self-rejection stems from his extreme thinking that insists on a clear, knowable distinction between what is morally right and wrong. Since humans are complex and contradictory beings, this desire for moral certainty is often a defense against our own thoughts and behaviors as we seek others to conform to a rigid moral order.[74] It is as if Harris wants to smuggle the logic of religious morality into the unbiased discourse of science so that he can have his dogmatism and anti-dogmatism at the same time.

## Right-Wing Scientism

It is important to stress that Harris not only wants to present neuroscience and evolutionary psychology as the only avenues for understanding the truth of human nature, but he also seeks to discredit the humanities and the social sciences as legitimate academic disciplines. Similar to Steven Pinker, this academic turf war is coupled with an attack on liberal tolerance, and in this way, we see the political nature of the new brain sciences.[75] Following the lead of the Neoliberal Right, the idea here is that it is the tolerant Left that allows the intolerant other to flourish. Once again, the desire for a purely objective and neutral scientific perspective is undermined by the injection of unconscious political prejudices shaped through denial, splitting, and projection.

Like so many other libertarians, Harris' unconscious investment in Right-wing beliefs is fueled in part by his inability to distinguish liberals from the Left.[76] Instead of seeing how liberals tend to reject the politics of the Left, he conflates the two: "The categorical distinction between facts and values has opened a sinkhole beneath secular liberalism—leading to moral relativism and masochistic depths of political correctness" (46). Although contemporary liberals often promote tolerance and multiculturalism, people on the Left practicing political correctness usually reject liberalism, and instead they often seek to impose their own moral order.[77] However, from the perspective of libertarian Right, there can be no difference between liberals and the Left because this would undermine the desire for a strict binary opposition between the good Right and the evil Left-liberal Other. We can see here how political polarization stems in part from the unconscious processes of denial, splitting, and projection; since we do not want to recognize our own aggression, we deny it, and we see the other as the aggressive one.[78] This type of thinking requires a zero-sum logic and a pure binary opposition because it cannot tolerate any ambiguity, complexity, or ambivalence. As a product of the pleasure principle, polarization seeks to avoid tension and conflict through splitting and the drawing of clear oppositional categories. Political polarization is then the social form of subjective splitting.[79]

What makes the new brain sciences fit into our neoliberal libertarian culture is that these discourses serve to make cultural and subjective opposition appear natural and inevitable: "We have good reason to believe that much of what we do in the name of 'morality' ... is borne of unconscious processes that were shaped by natural selection" (48–49). In this version of the unconscious, it is evolution that determines our morality and not culture or subjectivity. By returning to biological determinism, Harris is able to replace the social science, humanities, and psychoanalysis with the natural sciences as the only way to explain what makes us human.

## Notes

1 Samuels, Robert. *Psychoanalyzing the Politics of the New Brain Sciences*. Springer, 2017.
2 Harris, Sam. *The Moral Landscape: How Science Can Determine Human Values*. Simon and Schuster, 2011.
3 Tallis, Raymond. *Aping Mankind*. Routledge, 2016.
4 Misulia, Mark. "Aping Mankind: Neuromania, Darwinitis, and the Misrepresentation of Humanity." *First Things: A Monthly Journal of Religion and Public Life* 223 (2012): 65–67.
5 Rose, Nikolas, and Joelle M. Abi-Rached. *Neuro: The New Brain Sciences and the Management of the Mind*. Princeton University Press, 2013.
6 Samuels, Robert. "Drugging Discontent: Psychoanalysis, Drives, and the Governmental University Medical Pharmaceutical Complex (GUMP)." *Psychoanalyzing the Politics of the New Brain Sciences*. Palgrave Pivot, Cham, 2017. 115–136.
7 Wright, Colin. "A Spoonful Of Sugar: Medication and the Psychoanalytic Body." *Psychoanalysis, Culture & Society* (2020): 1–20.
8 Rose, Steven, Richard Charles Lewontin, and L. Kamin. "Not in Our Genes: Biology, Ideology and Human Nature." *The Wilson Quarterly* 152 (1984).
9 Williams, Richard N., and Daniel N. Robinson, eds. *Scientism: The New Orthodoxy*. Bloomsbury Publishing, 2014.
10 Freud, Sigmund. *Totem and Taboo: Some Points of Agreement between the Mental Lives of Savages and Neurotics*. WW Norton, 1989.
11 Hacker, P. M. S. "Philosophy and Scientism: What Cognitive Neuroscience Can, and What It Cannot, Explain." *Scientism: The New Orthodoxy*, 2015. 97–115.
12 Kaufman, Whitley R. P. "Can Science Determine Moral Values? A Reply to Sam Harris." *Neuroethics* 5.1 (2012): 55–65.
13 Lacan, Jacques. *The Four Fundamental Concepts of Psycho-Analysis*. Vol. 11. WW Norton, 1998.
14 Winthrop, Henry. "Scientism in Psychology." *Journal of Individual Psychology* 15.1 (1959): 112.
15 Allen, Tom, and Robin Widdison. "Can Computers Make Contracts." *Harv. JL & Tech.* 9 (1996): 25.
16 Mosco, Vincent. "Computers and Democracy." *The Information Society: Evolving Landscapes*. Springer, New YorK, 1990. 215–231.
17 Pykett, Jessica. *Brain Culture: Shaping Policy through Neuroscience*. Policy Press, 2015.
18 Klein, Ezra. "Sam Harris, Charles Murray, and the Allure of Race Science." *Vox, March* 27 (2018).
19 Samuels, Robert. "The Backlash Politics of Evolutionary Psychology: Steven Pinker's Blank Slate." *Psychoanalyzing the Politics of the New Brain Sciences*. Palgrave Pivot, Cham, 2017. 35–58.
20 Miller, Eleanor M., and Carrie Yang Costello. "The Limits of Biological Determinism." *American Sociological Review* 66.4 (2001): 592–598.
21 Luhrmann, Tanya Marie. "Beyond the Brain." *The Wilson Quarterly* 36.3 (2012): 28.
22 Gold, Sigfried. "Atheist Spirituality Hits the Big Time: A Review of Waking Up: A Guide to Spirituality without Religion by Sam Harris." *Skeptic (Altadena, CA)* 19.4 (2014): 60–64.
23 Blackaby, Mike. "A Worldview Analysis of Sam Harris' Philosophical Naturalism in The Moral Landscape: How Science Can Determine Human Values." (2016).

24  Wallace, B. Alan. *Contemplative Science: Where Buddhism and Neuroscience Converge*. Columbia University Press, 2009.
25  Lynch, Michael. "We Have Never Been Anti-Science: Reflections on Science Wars and Post-Truth." *Engaging Science, Technology, and Society* 6 (2020): 49–57.
26  Martí, Gerardo, Grace Yukich, and Penny Edgell. "White Christian Libertarianism and the Trump Presidency." *Religion Is Raced: Understanding American Religion in the Twenty-First Century*, 2020. 19.
27  Postman, Neil. *Amusing Ourselves to Death: Public Discourse in the Age of Show Business*. Penguin, 2006.
28  Kaufman, Whitley R. P. "Can Science Determine Moral Values? A Reply to Sam Harris." *Neuroethics* 5.1 (2012): 55–65.
29  Khan, Muqtedar. "New Atheists and the Same Old Islamophobia." *The Islamic Monthly* (2015): 29–31.
30  Schulzke, Marcus. "The Politics of New Atheism." *Politics & Religion* 6.4 (2013): 778–799.
31  Martinez, Mark Anthony. *The Myth of the Free Market: The Role of the State in a Capitalist Economy*. Kumarian Press, 2009.
32  Loose, Rik. *The Subject of Addiction: Psychoanalysis and the Administration of Enjoyment*. Routledge, 2018.
33  Wood, Ellen Meiksins. *The Origin of Capitalism: A Longer View*. Verso, 2002.
34  Markram, Henry. "Seven Challenges for Neuroscience." *Functional Neurology* 28.3 (2013): 145.
35  Gosling, Samuel D. "From Mice to Men: What Can We Learn about Personality from Animal Research?." *Psychological Bulletin* 127.1 (2001): 45.
36  Legrenzi, Paolo, and Carlo Umiltà. *Neuromania: On the Lmits of Brain Science*. Oxford University Press, 2011.
37  Nguyen-Phuong-Mai, Mai. "A Critical Analysis of Cultural Metaphors and Static Cultural Frameworks with Insight from Cultural Neuroscience and Evolutionary Biology." *Cross Cultural & Strategic Management* (2017).
38  Cowley, Stephen J., Frédéric Vallée-Tourangeau, and Frédéric Vallée-Tourangeau. *Cognition Beyond the Brain*. Springer International Publishing, 2017.
39  Lewontin, Richard, Steven Rose, and Leo Kamin. "Bourgeois Ideology and the Origins of Biological Determinism." *Race & Class* 24.1 (1982): 1–16.
40  Samuels, Robert. *New Media, Cultural Studies, and Critical Theory after Postmodernism: Automodernity from Zizek to Laclau*. Springer, 2009.
41  Zizek, Slavoj, ed. *Mapping Ideology*. Verso Books, 2012.
42  Thatcher, Margaret. "No Such Thing as Society." *Intervista per Woman's Own* 23 (1987).
43  Hoover, Kenneth R. "The Rise of Conservative Capitalism: Ideological Tensions within the Reagan and Thatcher Governments." *Comparative Studies in Society and History* 29.2 (1987): 245–268.
44  George, Susan. "A Short History of Neoliberalism." *Conference on Economic Sovereignty in a Globalising World*. Vol. 24. 1999.
45  Samuels, Robert. "The Brain Sciences against the Welfare State." *Psychoanalyzing the Politics of the New Brain Sciences*. Palgrave Pivot, Cham, 2017. 85–114.
46  Frank, Thomas. *One Market under God: Extreme Capitalism, Market Populism, and the End of Economic Democracy*. Anchor Canada, 2001.
47  Samuels, Robert. "Catharsis: The Politics of Enjoyment." *Zizek and the Rhetorical Unconscious*. Palgrave Macmillan, Cham, 2020. 7–31.
48  Smith, Richard J. "Darwin, Freud, and the Continuing Misrepresentation of the Primal Horde." *Current Anthropology* 57.6 (2016): 838–843.

49 Narveson, Jan. *The Libertarian Idea.* Broadview Press, 2001.
50 D'souza, Dinesh. *Illiberal Education: The Politics of Race and Sex on Campus.* Simon and Schuster, 1991.
51 Block, Walter. "A Libertarian Analysis of the COVID-19 Pandemic." *Journal of Libertarian Studies* 24.1 (2020): 206–237.
52 Winston, Andrew S. "Neoliberalism and IQ: Naturalizing Economic and Racial Inequality." *Theory & Psychology* 28.5 (2018): 600–618.
53 Freud, Sigmund. "Beyond the Pleasure Principle." *The Standard Edition of the Complete Psychological Works of Sigmund Freud, Volume XVIII (1920–1922): Beyond the Pleasure Principle, Group Psychology and Other Works.* 1955. 1–64.
54 Kahneman, Daniel. *Thinking, Fast and Slow.* Macmillan, 2011.
55 Samuels, Robert. "Science and the Reality Principle." *Freud for the Twenty-First Century.* Palgrave Pivot, Cham, 2019. 5–16.
56 Lacan, Jacques, Alan Sheridan, and Malcolm Bowie. "The Function and Field of Speech and Language in Psychoanalysis." *Écrits: A Selection.* Routledge, 2020. 33–125.
57 Perry, Mark. "Distributed Cognition." *HCI Models, Theories, and Frameworks: Toward a Multidisciplinary Science,* 2003. 193–223.
58 Hutchins, Edwin. "Distributed Cognition." *International Encyclopedia of the Social and Behavioral Sciences.* Elsevier Science 138 (2000).
59 Hoffman, Paul. "Descartes's Theory of Distinction." *Philosophy and Phenomenological Research* 64.1 (2002): 57–78.
60 Freud, Sigmund. *The Antithetical Meaning of Primal Words.* Read Books, 2014.
61 Freud, Sigmund. *Jokes and Their Relation to the Unconscious.* WW Norton, 1960.
62 Geertz, Clifford. "Distinguished Lecture: Anti Anti-relativism." *American Anthropologist* 86.2 (1984): 263–278.
63 Jaede, Riccardo. "The Epistemic Violence of Sam Harris' Doxastic Theory of Action in the End of Faith." *Muslims in the UK and Europe II* (2016): 54–65.
64 Mondon, Aurelien, and Aaron Winter. "Articulations of Islamophobia: from the Extreme to the Mainstream?." *Ethnic and Racial Studies* 40.13 (2017): 2151–2179.
65 Henkin, Louis. "Religion, Religions, and Human Rights." *The Journal of Religious Ethics* (1998): 229–239.
66 Lean, Nathan. "Dawkins, Harris, Hitchens: New Atheists Flirt with Islamophobia." *Salon. com* 30.3 (2013): 2013.
67 Ladyman, James. "Scientism with a Humane Face." *Scientism: Prospects and Problems,* 2018.
68 Kuhn, Thomas S. *The Structure of Scientific Revolutions.* University of Chicago Press, 2012.
69 Sandler, Joseph. *Projection, Identification, Projective Identification.* Routledge, 2018.
70 Perry, J. Christopher, and Steven H. Cooper. "A Preliminary Report on Defenses and Conflicts Associated with Borderline Personality Disorder." *Journal of the American Psychoanalytic Association* 34.4 (1986): 863–893.
71 Klein, Ezra. *Why We're Polarized.* Simon and Schuster, 2020.
72 Tawfik, A., and A. Diab. "Generalized Uncertainty Principle: Approaches and Applications." *International Journal of Modern Physics D* 23.12 (2014): 1430025.
73 Flanagan, Scott C., and Aie-Rie Lee. "The New Politics, Culture Wars, and the Authoritarian-libertarian Value Change in Advanced Industrial Democracies." *Comparative Political Studies* 36.3 (2003): 235–270.
74 Fromm, Erich. *Escape from Freedom.* Macmillan, 1994.
75 Samuels, Robert. "The Backlash Politics of Evolutionary Psychology: Steven Pinker's Blank Slate." *Psychoanalyzing the Politics of the New Brain Sciences.* Palgrave Pivot, Cham, 2017. 35–58.

76 Wallis, Jim. *God's politics: Why the Right Gets It Wrong and the Left Doesn't Get It*. Zondervan, 2005.
77 Pluckrose, Helen, and James A. Lindsay. *Cynical Theories: How Activist Scholarship Made Everything about Race, Gender, and Identity—and Why This Harms Everybody*. Pitchstone Publishing (US&CA), 2020.
78 Layton, Lynne, Nancy Caro Hollander, and Susan Gutwill, eds. *Psychoanalysis, Class and Politics: Encounters in the Clinical Setting*. Routledge, 2006.
79 Dervin, Dan. "Political Leaders and Psychohistorical Approaches in a Time of Borderline Polarization." *The Journal of psychohistory* 43.2 (2015): 89.

# Chapter 4

# Is Language an Instinct?

In the last chapter, I focused on how Sam Harris' work reveals the ways the new brain sciences often repress psychoanalysis as they block our ability to understand what makes us human. In this chapter, I will continue to look at the some of the same dynamics as they are represented in Steven Pinker's *The Language Instinct*.[1] A central aspect of this analysis will be to examine how biological models of the human mind often misunderstand what language is and does. This topic is so important because if we want to know what makes us human, we have to comprehend the true nature of symbolic representations and communication. Pinker's work helps to clarify this issue because his perspective is so clear and misguided.

## On Humans, Machines, and Animals

Like Harris, a large part of Pinker's discourse is centered on discrediting other academic disciplines as he seeks to find a natural and biological basis for human subjectivity and culture.[2] From the perspective of his scientism, the humanities, social sciences, and psychoanalysis have been surpassed by a combination of the cognitive sciences and evolutionary psychology:

> Some thirty-five years ago a new science was born. Now called "cognitive science," it combines tools from psychology, computer science, linguistics, philosophy, and neurobiology to explain the workings of human intelligence. The science of language, in particular, has seen spectacular advances in the years since. There are many phenomena of language that we are coming to understand nearly as well as we understand how a camera works or what the spleen is for. (3)

In this new effort to understand what makes us human, we will find the combination of the animal and the machine coupled with the repression of culture and unconscious subjectivity.[3] Instead of seeing language as a human invention, Pinker bases our linguistic abilities on biology.

DOI: 10.4324/9781003364610-4

Instead of seeing how language is learned and how it is affected by cultural differences and internal unconscious processes, Pinker wants to claim that language is a biological instinct hard-wired into our brains as a product of natural selection: "Language is not a cultural artifact that we learn the way we learn to tell time or how the federal government works. Instead, it is a distinct piece of the biological makeup of our brains" (4). By separating language from education, culture, and subjectivity, Pinker also reduces what makes us human through his application of an evolutionary imperative.[4] One of the results of this theory is that the importance of politics, history, education, and personal experience are downplayed—if not eliminated—as biological determinism serves to repress what makes us human.[5]

From the perspective of the cognitive unconscious, language is not learned; rather, we are born pre-wired with a linguistic instinct: "Language is a complex, specialized skill, which develops in the child spontaneously, without conscious effort or formal instruction, is deployed without awareness of its underlying logic, is qualitatively the same in every individual" (4). As a natural product of evolutionary determinism, Pinker argues that language is learned spontaneously without the need for instruction and without conscious understanding.[6] Although, Pinker is saying here that language is largely unconscious, his cognitive version of the unconscious has little to do with the psychoanalytic conception of the unconscious.[7] For him, language is unconscious because it is a universal product of biology shaped through evolution, and it comes hard-wired in our brains and thus does not have to rely on culture or subjectivity. As an information-processing machine, this natural instinct is represented by metaphors dealing with animals and machines.[8] In fact, we can think of the language instinct as the foundation of a mechanical animal void of social and psychological differences. Clearly, this approach prevents us from seeing what makes us human because it is centered on the nonhuman as an explanatory lens.

## Instincts and Evolution

As I have previously stressed, one of the things that makes us different from other animals is that we are not determined by our instincts since we can make anything an object of pleasure, and yet Pinker wants to insist that we are driven by instincts: "It conveys the idea that people know how to talk in more or less the sense that spiders know how to spin webs" (5). From this perspective, not only is our subjectivity and sexuality void of free will, but language itself is a pure product of nature.[9] Just as spiders do not have to be taught how to spin a web, children do not have to be instructed in how to use language since they are born with a spontaneous ability to communicate in a coherent way. Anyone who has ever had to raise a child should be shocked by this claim, but we shall see how Pinker tries to make his counter-intuitive case.[10]

To prove his argument, Pinker has to first dismiss other disciplines so that he can show that only his brand of evolutionary cognitive science can explain the truth: "Thinking of language as an instinct inverts the popular wisdom, especially as it has been passed down in the canon of the humanities and social sciences. Language is no more a cultural invention than is upright posture" (5). By comparing the learning and use of language to a person's physical posture, Pinker seeks to base linguistics on biology and not culture, subjectivity, history, or politics.

Not only does Pinker want to separate language from culture, but he also wants to separate it from thought:

> Once you begin to look at language not as the ineffable essence of human uniqueness but as a biological adaptation to communicate information, it is no longer as tempting to see language as an insidious shaper of thought, and, we shall see, it is not. (5)

Language is thus represented as a mental process determined by evolution and distinct from human thought. From this perspective, it is wrong for people to think that our perceptions of the world and our own selves are shaped by our linguistic categories; instead, language is a set of pre-programmed rules and symbols similar to a computer.[11] However, while a computer has to be programmed and the data has to be inputted, for Pinker, humans are a machine that does not need any external help. This privileging of nature over nurture is expressed when he writes that "as Oscar Wilde said, 'Education is an admirable thing, but it is well to remember from time to time that nothing that is worth knowing can be taught'" (6). This reference to the impossibility of teaching anyone anything is very paradoxical because it comes from a professor and public intellectual whose entire career is shaped by education. After all, why would Pinker write anything at all if he thought that people could not be taught?[12]

Perhaps Pinker only intends to say that our ability to use language is pre-wired into our brain, but the content has to be learned from experience. However, we shall see that he turns to evolutionary psychology to argue that it is not just the hardware that comes from nature but much of the software and content is also derived from natural selection.[13] Thus, he uses Darwin to explain the origins of the language instinct: "Darwin concluded that language ability is "an instinctive tendency to acquire an art," a design that is not peculiar to humans but seen in other species such as song-learning birds" (6). Once again, we find here the tendency to compare human language to the instinctual sounds of non-human animals. Thus, instead of seeing how our use of language relies on symbols that are complex, ambiguous, and over-determined, Pinker needs to represent our symbolic systems as transparent and one-dimensional as the songs produced by birds.[14]

## What Makes Our Language Human?

If language is one of the things that makes us human, it is essential to understand how our use of language differs from other animals, and yet, Pinker is dedicated to the principle that language is a purely instinctual entity. Furthermore, due to its biological and evolutionary nature, human language is presented as being separated from conscious awareness: "The workings of language are as far from our awareness as the rationale for egg-laying is from the fly's" (8). Once again, it by repressing what makes us human that Pinker is able to compare us to other beings that do not have culture, language, or subjectivity.[15] This argument appears to be so absurd, but we shall see that it is becoming increasingly popular with the growing influence of neuroscience, evolutionary psychology, computer science, and cognitive psychology.

It should be clear that Pinker's theory of language is not only anti-psychoanalytic, but it is also anti-social. Since he does not think that language can be taught or that parents can help their children learn, he challenges many of the core principles that shape modern democratic life.[16] For instance, in the following passage, he rejects the idea that people learn through imitation and education: "We think children pick up their mother tongue by imitating their mothers, but when a child says Don't giggle me! or We holded the baby rabbits, it cannot be an act of imitation" (8). This rejection of imitation as one of the foundations of language learning and comprehension leads to a rejection of modern rationality and science since reason is based on the ability of people to learn new things that go against their instinctual impulses.[17] Also, just because people can talk fluently or think that their words are perfectly transparent does not mean that language is actually clearly understood by others and by our own selves. Although, people can use language to communicate their ideas to other people, they also can misunderstand each other and lie to themselves. Moreover, even if we act as if our words are transparent and others are internalizing our exact intentions, people constantly misunderstand others, and our words often have multiple, conflicting meanings.[18] And while we sometimes avoid our own internalized social censors, people often repress what they want to say or say things in an indirect, symbolic way.[19]

Pinker has to reduce the complexity of language because he needs to see it as a transparent medium shaped by pre-determined programs inherited through natural selection. Following Chomsky, he insists that grammar is a universal program derived from evolution: "That program may be called a mental grammar (not to be confused with pedagogical or stylistic 'grammars,' which are just guides to the etiquette of written prose)" (9). By combining theories of information processing with biological models of animal instinctual behavior, Pinker wants to show that language must be a universal system derived from natural selection:

The second fundamental fact is that children develop these complex grammars rapidly and without formal instruction and grow up to give consistent interpretations to novel sentence constructions that they have never before encountered. Therefore, he argued, children must innately be equipped with a plan common to the grammars of all languages, a Universal Grammar, that tells them how to distill the syntactic patterns out of the speech of their parents. (9)

Since children are able to detect and utilize complicated grammatical structures at an early age, Pinker and Chomsky argue that this ability to utilize language must be universal and therefore a biological product of evolution.[20] Even if people have different language abilities and distinct cultures have different grammatical structures, Pinker posits that they all share the same basic ingredients, and so these elements must have come from the same source.

According to the logic of evolutionary psychology, any human aspect that is universal and intuitive is the product of natural selection, and therefore it does not matter if we are talking about physical traits or mental states:[21]

It is taken for granted that the physical structure of the organism is genetically determined ... Why, then, should we not study the acquisition of a cognitive structure such as language more or less as we study some complex bodily organ? (9)

Just as evolutionary psychologists and neuroscientists tend to equate the brain with the mind, they also want to repress the differences between physical and mental development. In an effort to deny the influence of education, culture, parenting, experience, history, and unconscious processes, Pinker ends up insisting that there is a universal human nature derived from laws of evolutionary biology.[22] From this perspective, even if we can show how languages have different grammatical structures, we can prove that there is some set of common mental programs shaping everyone's use of language.

## Why Words Matter

One reason why I am spending so much time quoting Pinker directly is that I want to show that in contrast to his theory, words really do matter, and they can shape how we see ourselves and the world around us. For example, by equating the words "mind" and "brain," he is able to switch between two very different aspects of human life.[23] Furthermore, the flexibility of language helps him to make an argument that is inherently self-contradictory. After all, why would he write about language if he thought that we can learn nothing through imitation or experience?

From Freud's perspective, a core moment in the development of human language occurs when a child cries, and a parent responds by providing attention and care in the form of satisfying unmet needs.[24] Lacan adds that what the child is really demanding is love, knowledge, and recognition, and this fundamental demand shapes the way we interact with other people on an unconscious level.[25] Ultimately, the demand of the child can never be fully satisfied, and so a desire is produced. Moreover, the demand represents a transference of responsibility from the child to the parent who is now charged with satisfying the pleasure principle for the child.[26] Fundamentally, what the child really wants is for the parent to sacrifice his or her own freedom to the freedom of the demanding subject. Since the child demands that the parent make suffering and un-pleasure go away, the parent is placed in an impossible situation since desire can never be fully satisfied.[27]

Freud adds that the roots of communication and social morality are derived from this relationship between the child's demand and the parent's response. Since the only way that the parent can help the child realize the goal of the pleasure principle is by understanding what the child wants, the parent has to recognize the meaning of the demand and act from a position of care and understanding. Transference then is a key aspect to human language, and the desire for knowledge, love, and recognition cannot be explained through a purely biological process since it requires a social interaction based on the illusion of symbolic transparency and shared understanding. Psychoanalysis therefore tells us that one of the things that makes us human is that we meditate our relationship with others through a shared system of symbolic communication, which is open to deception, idealization, identification, and misrecognition.[28] In fact, the child's demand has multiple meanings and does not point to a purely transparent use of language.

Since Pinker wants to see language as an instinct comparable to the information processing of computers, he has no reason to bother with the complexity of the human demand. Thus, he constantly utilizes metaphors borrowed from technology in order to explain how human language works: "Ordinary speech, like color vision or walking, is a paradigm of engineering excellence—a technology that works so well that the user takes its outcome for granted, unaware of the complicated machinery hidden behind the panels" (15). As we learn from psychoanalysis, the metaphors that people use often confuse correlation with causation.[29] Since the human mind processes experience by making association between things that have no natural or real connection, we are able to transcend reality, but this aspect of mental autonomy also makes us prone to confuse facts with imaginary constructions.[30] However, due to Pinker's desire to see language as a transparent medium, he does not have to bother with the complexity of our modes of communication and thought. Moreover, psychoanalysis tells us that we do see the world through social categories and shared symbols, and so consciousness itself is structured by language.[31]

## The Universal Machine of Nature

Although, Pinker does not deny the fact that there are different languages with different words and concepts, his focus is on seeing language as a universal program representing shared functions and processes: "When speakers of different languages have to communicate to carry out practical tasks but do not have the opportunity to learn one another's languages, they develop a makeshift jargon called a pidgin" (15). Pinker's point here is that even if people do not share the same linguistic system, they can still communicate with each other by using signs that can be understood by anyone.[32] In other words, languages enable us to get things done in the world, and these actions are shaped by a shared set of mental categories; therefore, it does not matter what words we use if others can understand what we are trying to say. However, Pinker also wants to move beyond the pragmatic conception of language by pointing to universal aspects of language that appear to serve no direct function: "The universal constraints on grammatical rules also show that the basic form of language cannot be explained away as the inevitable outcome of a drive for usefulness" (31). Pinker's main point here is that our language instinct is not purely based on the need to solve shared human problems; rather, we have inherited universal mental concepts and logical structures.[33] This jump from the biological to the mental is not explained here, but we shall see that he does try to provide a theory of how thoughts are shaped by nature.

Since neuroscientists and evolutionary psychology often want to base human thought on evolution, they have to relate genes to specific brain structures, which, in turn, produce particular mental states: "If language is an instinct, it should have an identifiable seat in the brain, and perhaps even a special set of genes that help wire it into place" (34). While Pinker wants to equate specific genes with particular neural structures resulting in specific mental processes, Freud, in his "Project for a Scientific Psychology," equates neurons with memories, thoughts, and symbols.[34] Just as a symbol always points to something else in a network of other symbols, memories only take on meaning in relation to other memories. In fact, the way Freud discusses neurons, it is clear that he is actually talking about signifiers since he understands them as being structured by their connections between other neurons and the differences between each neuron.[35] As an anticipation of structural linguistics, Freud thus reveals how human biological entities, like neurons, have to be understood as symbolic structures since each element only has a meaning in relation to other elements. Although, he began as a neurologist and at first tried to use biological and chemical terms to describe mental processes, he quickly moved to basing human thought on symbolic networks and not on inherited natural components. As Lacan was fond of saying, a signifier can never signify itself because one signifier always represents its subject for another signifier.[36] Due to the fact that words are symbols, they do not have any meaning in themselves because a symbol always points to something else.

## Repressing the Symbolic

Since Pinker and other neuroscientists and evolutionary psychologists need to relate language to a universal biology, they have to repress the symbolic aspects of discourse in order to reduce words to a transparent medium.[37] Just as Harris wants to find a universal morality centered on the brain, Pinker also desires to reject any form of cultural relativism so that he can affirm a non-cultural, totalizing interpretation of language:

> People who remember little else from their college education can rattle off the factoids: the languages that carve the spectrum into color words at different places, the fundamentally different Hopi concept of time, the dozens of Eskimo words for snow. The implication is heavy: the foundational categories of reality are not "in" the world but are imposed by one's culture (and hence can be challenged, perhaps accounting for the perennial appeal of the hypothesis to undergraduate sensibilities). (45)

As his sarcastic tone implies, Pinker mocks the idea that culture shapes our perceptions of the world.[38] Furthermore, because he needs to denounce cultural relativism and social constructionism in order to preserve his universal biological model, he spends a great amount of time trying to show how particular languages do not result in particular views of reality. Just as many Right-wing intellectuals define themselves against the postmodern conceptions of cultural relativism and social constructivism, Pinker seeks to reject the importance of culture, history, education, and social mediation.[39] By fusing his discourse on the animal and the computer, he clears a space to efface the social as a defining aspect of the human. This rejection of the social can be read as a political ideology bent on devaluing the need for being sensitive to minority cultures and individual differences. From this perspective, it is not only what Pinker says that is important, but it is also vital to look at what he does not say and excludes through his rhetoric.

Although, Pinker wants to deny the power of words to shape human perceptions, his own discourse is determined by how he manipulates words to produce a certain effect in his reader's mind.[40] Therefore, one way that he is able to try to convince people that language is an instinct is through his choice of metaphors and other figures of speech. Of course, his theory downplays these symbolic aspects, but his own writing acts as a return of the repressed. After all, in order to present his objective scientific facts, he cannot help but to rely on metaphors that function by substituting one thing for another.[41] Just as he replaces the mind with the brain, he also replaces the human with the animal. These very different things are able to be treated as the same because language gives us the ability to replace difference with identity. In fact, Freud argued that the primary processes shaping the unconscious function through substitution (metaphor) and association (metonymy).[42] For instance, everything you see in a dream actually represents something else, and one dream image can relate to multiple other memories.[43] Perhaps these automatic mental processes are inherited, but what cannot be the result of biological endowment is the specific words and meanings that an individual experiences.

Since our consciousness itself is defined by thought, and thought is structured through symbolic memory, the way we perceive reality is shaped by substitution and displacement. Furthermore, our inability to know at any moment if we are dreaming or awake means that our thoughts transcend reality, and their reliance on symbolism indicates that we are not in control of our own thoughts. What Freud, then, found in dreams was the presence of an automatic system of representation, which was not controlled by the intentions of the ego or an evolutionary instinct. Instead, primary processes shape our consciousness, which means that we do not intend or plan our own thoughts.[44] To prove this point, one can simply follow the flow of one's own thinking, and then ask if the stream of consciousness was planned or controlled.[45] One can also take hallucinogenic drugs or meditate to discover the absence of the ego; in other words, we are not always in control of our own thoughts, and these thoughts shape our consciousness.[46]

From Freud's perspective, psychotics, dreamers, infants, and animistic cultures are all determined by the confusion between thoughts and reality.[47] However, I am arguing here that our normal consciousness also partakes in this confusion since our thoughts are symbols, and there is no clear separation between false memories and perceptions of reality. Moreover, what then makes something unconscious is not that it is automatic and determined by nature; what the psychoanalytic unconscious is based on is the repression of thoughts and their replacement with intentions controlled by the ego.[48] As Freud insisted, we are not born with an ego, and this sense of being a separate person is developed through a process of identification triggered by a set of brain developments.[49] Lacan added that the child around two years of age will recognize itself in the mirror and will identify with the image, and this external representation is then internalized as a virtual body map.[50] Once again, reality is transcended when one internalizes the identification with an external representation.

## The Ego and the Unconscious

The formation of the ego allows for consciousness to be repressed and turned into unconsciousness as the ego injects intentionality into awareness. What is often missing in dreams, hallucinations, and deep meditation is the ego itself, and this is why so many different spiritual practices see the self as an illusion.[51] By suspending the ego, one is able to be absorbed in thought associations without any sense of control. For instance, if someone lies in a deprivation tank, they can begin to hallucinate, and they have no control over what they are seeing or thinking.[52] Since this process functions by eliminating perceptions of the external world, they are similar to the dream state where one removes oneself from the world by closing one's eyes and suspending the normal ego functions.[53] The fact that we can enter this state by simply removing the perception of external sensations shows that our intentional ego is built around the control of internal and external perceptions.[54]

Like so many evolutionary psychologists and neuroscientists, Pinker's cognitive science has no need for consciousness or even unconsciousness, and this repression of what makes us human is motivated in part by a desire to deny the role that socio-symbolic representations play in shaping our thoughts and language use:

> The idea that language shapes thinking seemed plausible when scientists were in the dark about how thinking works or even how to study it. Now that cognitive scientists know how to think about thinking, there is less of a temptation to equate it with language just because words are more palpable than thoughts. (48)

From the perspective of brain scientism, we finally know what defines language, and it has nothing to do with words.[55]

To show that mental thoughts are not dependent on words, Pinker points out that many thinkers see images when they are discovering something new (61). What Pinker misses here is that the images in dreams and hallucinations function as symbols since they are signs for something else and function on a figurative, metaphorical level.[56] As symbolic representations, words and dream images are not direct perceptions of the visual world; rather dream images are always related to other ideas, and thus their meaning has to be traced through a network of symbolic associations.[57]

## Mechanical Language

Pinker's endeavor to remove society and symbolic mediation from language is coupled with the use of mechanical metaphors to describe how people use language: "To get reasoning to happen, we now need a processor ... For example, imagine a machine that can move around on a printed page" (65). This passage is very telling because it shows how cognitive scientists have helped to usher in the age of computer technology through their transformation of thought and language into mechanical processes.[58] However, it is important to remember that thinking machines actually do not think or understand anything.[59] Also, these computers do not have any free will, and they are completely dependent on data and programs that are inputted by humans. Even if computers can program other computers or can provide data for other machines, we still have to locate a human using language and free will at the start of the process.

Pinker is at times aware that there is a world of difference between humans and computers, and yet he constantly returns to this analogy in order to define the essence of language. Furthermore, according to evolutionary psychology, humans are computers programmed by natural selection, but what this theory misses is the notion that humans do have egos, and they do at least try to understand themselves and each other.[60] When we remove understanding from language, we are simply left with the processing of information through predetermined logical relationships. This view of the human mind denies our humanness by eliminating free will, consciousness, and intentionality.

## Notes

1 Pinker, Steven. *The Language Instinct: How the Mind Creates Language*. Penguin UK, 2003.
2 Samuels, Robert. "The Backlash Politics of Evolutionary Psychology: Steven Pinker's Blank Slate." *Psychoanalyzing the Politics of the New Brain Sciences*. Palgrave Pivot, Cham, 2017. 35–58.
3 Clark, Andy. *Mindware: An Introduction to the Philosophy of Cognitive Science*. Oxford University Press, 2000.
4 Gleitman, Lila R., and Elissa L. Newport. "The Invention of Language by Children: Environmental and Biological Influences on the Acquisition of Language." *An Invitation to Cognitive Science* 1 (1995): 1–24.
5 Lewontin, Richard C., Steven Rose, and Leon J. Kamin. *Not in Our Genes*. New York, Pantheon Books, 1984.
6 Scott-Phillips, Thomas C. "Evolutionary Psychology and the Origins of Language: (Editorial for the special issue of Journal of Evolutionary Psychology on the evolution of language)." *Journal of Evolutionary Psychology* 8.4 (2010): 289–307.
7 Eagle, Morris N. "The Psychoanalytic and the Cognitive Unconscious." (1987).
8 Dehaene, Stanislas, Hakwan Lau, and Sid Kouider. "What Is Consciousness, and Could Machines Have It?." *Science* 358.6362 (2017): 486–492.
9 Sampson, Geoffrey. "There Is No Language Instinct." *Ilha do Desterro: A Journal of English Language, Literatures in English and Cultural Studies* 52 (2007): 35–63.
10 Yusa, Noriaki, et al. "Second-Language Instinct and Instruction Effects: Nature and Nurture in Second-language Acquisition." *Journal of Cognitive Neuroscience* 23.10 (2011): 2716–2730.
11 Cowley, Stephen J. "The Baby, the Bathwater and the "Language Instinct" Debate." *Language Sciences* 23.1 (2001): 69–91.
12 Sampson, Geoffrey. *Educating Eve*. Cassell, London, 1997.
13 Zidong, Huang. "Review of Pinker's the Language Instinct [J]." *Modern Foreign Languages* 1 (1998).
14 Zyzik, Eve. "The 'Language Instinct' Debate: Revised Edition." (2007): 134–136.
15 Nordlund, David EC. "Language as Instinct: A Socio-Cultural Perspective (a review essay) The Language Instinct: How the Mind Creates Language by Steven Pinker. New York: William Morrow, 1994. pp. 494." *Issues in Applied Linguistics* 7.2 (1996).

16  Tomasello, Michael. "Language Is Not an Instinct." (1995): 131–156.
17  Bloom, Lois, Lois Hood, and Patsy Lightbown. "Imitation in Language Development: If, When, and Why." *Cognitive Psychology* 6.3 (1974): 380–420.
18  Schober, Michael F., Frederick G. Conrad, and Scott S. Fricker. "Misunderstanding Standardized Language in Research Interviews." *Applied Cognitive Psychology* 18.2 (2004): 169–188.
19  Billig, Michael. *Freudian repression: Conversation Creating the Unconscious.* Cambridge University Press, 1999.
20  Sinha, Sweta. "Biological Basis of Language Revisited: A Review of Steven Pinker's The Language Instinct (1994) USA: William Morrow and Company."
21  Samuels, Robert. "The Brain Sciences against the Welfare State." *Psychoanalyzing the Politics of the New Brain Sciences.* Palgrave Pivot, Cham, 2017. 85–114.
22  Scott, Robert Ian. "Do Words and the Rest of our Behavior Affect Each Other? A Critical Response to 'The Language Instinct'." *ETC.: A Review of General Semantics* 53.2 (1996): 170–173.
23  Marler, Peter. "A Dynamic Systems Approach to Development: Applications; The Language Instinct." (1995): 101–109.
24  Freud, Sigmund. "Project for a Scientific Psychology (1950 [1895])." *The Standard Edition of the Complete Psychological Works of Sigmund Freud, Volume I (1886–1899): Pre-Psycho-Analytic Publications and Unpublished Drafts,* 1966. 281–391.
25  Epstein, Charlotte. "The Productive force of the Negative and the Desire for Recognition: Lessons from Hegel and Lacan." *Review of International Studies* 44.5 (2018): 805–828.
26  Samuels, Robert. "Transference and Narcissism." *Freud for the Twenty-First Century.* Palgrave Pivot, Cham, 2019. 43–51.
27  Boothby, Richard. *Death and Desire (RLE: Lacan): Psychoanalytic Theory in Lacan's Return to Freud.* Routledge, 2014.
28  Huson, Timothy. "Truth and Contradiction: Reading Hegel with Lacan." *Lacan: The Silent Partners.* London, Verso, 2006.
29  Freud, Sigmund. *Psychopathology of Everyday Life.* Penguin books, 1938.
30  Vikan, Arne, and Sten Erik Clausen. "Freud, Piaget, or Neither? Beliefs in Controlling Others by Wishful Thinking and Magical Behavior in Young Children." *The Journal of Genetic Psychology* 154.3 (1993): 297–314.
31  Bracher, Mark. *Lacan, Discourse, and Social Change: A Psychoanalytic Cultural Criticism.* Cornell University Press, 1993.
32  Nordlund, David EC. "Language as Instinct: A Socio-Cultural Perspective (a review essay) The Language Instinct: How." *Issue: Issues in Applied Linguistics* 7.2 (1996).
33  LaPolla, Randy J. "Evans, Vyvyan. 2014. The Language Myth: Why Language Is Not an Instinct." *Studies in Language. International Journal sponsored by the Foundation "Foundations of Language"* 40.1 (2016): 235–252.
34  Woody, J. Melvin, and James Phillips. "Freud's 'Project for a Scientific Psychology' after 100 years: The Unconscious Mind in the Era of Cognitive Neuroscience." *Philosophy, Psychiatry, & Psychology* 2.2 (1995): 123–134.
35  Derrida, Jacques, and Jeffrey Mehlman. "Freud and the Scene of Writing." *Yale French Studies* 48 (1972): 74–117.
36  Miller, Jacques-Alain, Paul Verhaeghe, and Ellie Ragland. *Jacques Lacan and the Other Side of Psychoanalysis: Reflections on Seminar XVII, sic vi.* Vol. 6. Duke University Press, 2006.
37  Donald, Davidson. "Seeing through Language." *Thought and Language* 15 (1997): 27.

38 Pinker, Steven. *The Blank Slate: The Modern Denial of Human Nature*. Penguin, 2003.

39 Ore, Tracy E., and Paul Kurtz. *The Social Construction of Difference and Inequality*. Mayfield Publishing, 2000.

40 Samuels, Robert. *Zizek and the Rhetorical Unconscious: Global Politics, Philosophy, and Subjectivity*. Springer Nature, 2020.

41 Semino, Elena. *Metaphor in Discourse*. Cambridge: Cambridge University Press, 2008.

42 Lacan, Jacques, Alan Sheridan, and Malcolm Bowie. "The Function and Field of Speech and Language in Psychoanalysis." *Écrits: A Selection*. Routledge, 2020. 33–125.

43 Freud, Sigmund, and A. J. Cronin. *The Interpretation of Dreams*. Read Books, 2013.

44 Freud, Sigmund. "A Metapsychological Supplement to the Theory of Dreams." *The Standard Edition of the Complete Psychological Works of Sigmund Freud, Volume XIV (1914–1916): On the History of the Psycho-Analytic Movement, Papers on Metapsychology and Other Works*, 1957. 217–235.

45 Christoff, Kalina, et al. "Mind-Wandering as Spontaneous Thought: A Dynamic Framework." *Nature Reviews Neuroscience* 17.11 (2016): 718–731.

46 Seli, Paul, et al. "Mind-Wandering with and without Intention." *Trends in Cognitive Sciences* 20.8 (2016): 605–617.

47 Freud, Sigmund. *Totem and Taboo: Resemblances between the Psychic Lives of Savages and Neurotics*. Good Press, 2019.

48 Freud, Sigmund. *Totem and Taboo: Resemblances between the Psychic Lives of Savages and Neurotics*. Good Press, 2019.

49 Freud, Sigmund. *On Narcissism: An Introduction*. Read Books, 2014.

50 Lacan, Jacques. "The Mirror Stage as Formative of the Function of the I as Revealed in Psychoanalytic Experience." *Cultural Theory and Popular Culture. A Reader* (1949): 287–292.

51 Thompson, Evan. *Waking, Dreaming, Being: Self and Consciousness in Neuroscience, Meditation, and Philosophy*. Columbia University Press, 2014.

52 Pierre, Joseph M. "Hallucinations in Nonpsychotic Disorders: Toward a Differential Diagnosis of "Hearing Voices"." *Harvard Review of Psychiatry* 18.1 (2010): 22–35.

53 Davis, John M., William F. McCourt, and Philip Solomon. "The Effect of Visual Stimulation on Hallucinations and Other Mental Experiences during Sensory Deprivation." *American Journal of Psychiatry* 116.10 (1960): 889–892.

54 Lichtenberg, Joseph. "The Testing of Reality from the Standpoint of the Body Self." *Journal of the American Psychoanalytic Association* 26.2 (1978): 357–385.

55 Jackendoff, Ray, and Ray S. Jackendoff. *Foundations of Language: Brain, Meaning, Grammar, Evolution*. Oxford University Press, USA, 2002.

56 Henshilwood, Christopher S., and Francesco d'Errico, eds. *Homo Symbolicus: The Dawn of Language, Imagination and Spirituality*. John Benjamins Publishing, 2011.

57 Fromm, Erich. *The Forgotten Language: An Introduction to the Understanding of Dreams, Fairy Tales, and Myths*. Open Road Media, 2013.

58 Gleick, James. "The Information: A History, a Theory, a Flood (Gleick, J.; 2011) [Book Review]." *IEEE Transactions on Information Theory* 57.9 (2011): 6332–6333.

59 Turing, Alan M. "Can Digital Computers Think?." *The Turing Test: Verbal Behavior as the Hallmark of Intelligence*, 1951.

60 Barrett, Louise, Thomas V. Pollet, and Gert Stulp. "From Computers to Cultivation: Reconceptualizing Evolutionary Psychology." *Frontiers in Psychology* 5 (2014): 867.

# Chapter 5

# Is Your Mind an iPhone? Replacing Humanity with the Machine

In *From Bacteria to Bach and Back: The Evolution of Minds*, Daniel Dennett develops many of the same ideas about the human mind that we have found in Harris and Pinker, but his work adds a special twist.[1] We shall see that his application of evolutionary psychology to the question of what makes us human forces us to think about the limits of artificial intelligence and the reasons why we are very different from computers. Although his work appears to eliminate the human from humanity, I will argue that his own theory ends up proving the opposite of what he wants to say.

## Why Do Minds Exist?

Dennett begins his analysis by asking the fundamental question of why do we have minds in the first place: "The short answer is that minds evolved and created thinking tools that eventually enabled minds to know how minds evolved, and even to know how these tools enabled them to know what minds are" (3). Similar to Pinker, Dennett sees the human mind as a tool produced through natural selection. Moreover, he combines evolution, functionalism, and computer science as he defines language as the extraction and manipulation of information for defined purposes.[2]

A key concept for Dennett is the notion of feedback, which he uses to describe how the human mind expands by reflecting on itself:

> Douglas Hofstadter's book, *I Am a Strange Loop* (2007), describes a mind composing itself in cycles of processing that loop around, twisting and feeding on themselves, creating exuberant reactions to reflections to reminders to reevaluations that generate novel structures: ideas, fantasies, theories, and, yes, thinking tools to create still more. (10)

The complexity of the human mind is thus in part determined by the way it reflects on itself in a series of self-contained loops or feedback mechanisms.[3] In other words, the human mind is self-reflexive and therefore self-creating. However, there are two twists to Dennett's description of metacognition: the

DOI: 10.4324/9781003364610-5

first is that this is a biological process found throughout nature, and the second is that it is a mechanical procedure: "Yes, we have a soul, but it's made of lots of tiny robots!" (13). Here we see how the ultimate goal of his argument is to show why we are nothing but robots, and therefore we lack free will, consciousness, and understanding.[4]

To prove his point, Dennett first performs a common misreading of Descartes' division between the mental and the physical: "he concluded that minds like his (and yours) were not material entities, like lungs or brains, but made of some second kind of stuff that didn't have to obey the laws of physics" (13). Like so many other readers of Descartes, Dennett wants to reduce complicated arguments to a simple binary dualism between the mind and the body.[5] The problem with this interpretation is that it ignores most of what Descartes says about humans. Although, Descartes does argue that the human mind can transcend material reality, he also posits that we never know if we are awake or dreaming, and so we never know if our thoughts point to real or imaginary things.[6] Complicating matters is that he defines reason as the ability to distinguish the true from the false, but he adds the only way science can approach the real is to apply the artificial order of math and logic.[7] Another problem that Descartes highlights is that we often conform to the action and ideas of others to escape feelings of guilt and anxiety, but this conformity results in us being ignorant of our own beliefs, and even when we do know what we believe, we often do not say it out of fear of social censorship.[8] The human subject that Descartes presents is thus much more complicated and contradictory than philosophers like Dennett admit. It is therefore hard to say that Descartes makes a clear divide between the mind and the body if nothing is really clear for Descartes.[9]

One reason why Dennett desires to see Descartes as a strict dualist is that he wants to eliminate human consciousness by arguing that there is nothing beyond the material, physical world: "The problem with dualism, ever since Descartes, is that nobody has ever been able to offer a convincing account of how these postulated interactive transactions between mind and body could occur without violating the laws of physics" (14). What is so contradictory about Dennett's argument here is that he is claiming that only physical laws should be able to explain what is not physical.[10] Yet, since there is no way of using physics to jump from the physical to the mental, the mental has to be understood as being physical. Here we lose the human break from biology and material reality since Dennett thinks everything can be reduced to physical laws.[11]

As we saw in my analysis of Pinker's work, one of the ways that these scientists break with the scientific method is that they show a lack of awareness to their own language. Since as Descartes insisted, the first step of the scientific method is to remove all bias through critical introspection, what makes Dennett's science unscientific is its lack of self-reflection, which is ironic since he wants to base his theory of the human mind on its self-reflexive properties.[12] This repression of self-reflexivity with a theory of reflexivity brings us to the psychoanalytic notion that it is not just important what one says, but we also have to think about the ways someone says something.[13] From this perspective, we should not only look at the metaphors Dennett uses but also examine the contradictory nature of his own discourse. How is it possible that he defines the human mind by its self-reflective nature, while he does not reflect on the nature of his own rhetoric?

## The Mind Is the Brain

Like Harris and Pinker, a key rhetorical move Dennett makes is to equate the mind with the brain: "Francis Crick ... argued that dualism is false; the mind just is the brain, a material organ with no mysterious extra properties not found in other living organisms" (14). In referring to a respected scientist, Dennett tries to borrow ethos from Crick in a process we can call credibility through association. This common rhetorical move relies on the magical processes of transferring value from one entity to the other by simply conjuring a known name that comes with a certain social authority.[14] Since people know that Crick is an important and respected scientist, any reference to his work helps the writer gain a sense of social acceptance. In short, if the "co-discoverer" of DNA says that the mind is just a brain, then it must be true.

In fact, Dennett employs a series of rhetorical devices to persuade his audience that the mind and the brain are the same thing, and therefore consciousness and free will do not really exist:

> If "we are just machines," what happens to free will and responsibility? How could our lives have meaning at all if we are just huge collections of proteins and other molecules churning away according to the laws of chemistry and physics? If moral precepts were nothing but extrusions generated by the hordes of microbiological nano-machines between our ears, how could they make a difference worth honoring?" (15)

While Dennett raises these important issues in the form of rhetorical questions, he never directly answers them, and instead, he returns to the notion that we are simply automatic machines preprogrammed by natural selection. Furthermore, it is my contention that his mode of scientism is actually a reactionary political ideology dressed up as an objective analysis of objective facts.

## Reactionary Scientism

From a Right-wing backlash perspective, it is beneficial to remove people from feelings of guilt and shame for social and economic inequality by telling them that they are not responsible.[15] Thus, according to the libertarian notion of the free market, we are only parts of a larger system that transcends our individual thinking, and so we can never fully understand the structure, and therefore there is no reason to resist or change it. Moreover, if the system is based on a bottom-up invisible hand where people contribute to the common good by acting on their own self-interest, then what appears to be free will is actually just a part of a larger unknowable process.[16] Also, if we are robots programmed by natural selection, then we are not responsible for our addictions or destructive actions and speech, and we should not resist the replacement of human workers with machines because after all, we are only machines ourselves.[17]

Although it may look like I may be projecting political ideas onto Dennett's discourse, it is important to realize how our words and ideas can affect other people in unintended ways and how our rhetoric can be the result of unknowingly imitating external ideas we have internalized on an unconscious basis.[18] Even if Dennett hates libertarianism, his theory can help support this ideology if it convinces people that they are just machines without responsibility.[19] In fact, Freud defines the pleasure principle as the human drive to escape tension, which often requires removing feelings of guilt, shame, and anxiety by denying responsibility for our own thoughts, words, and actions.[20] Intentionally or unintentionally, Dennett follows Harris and Pinker in feeding the logic of the libertarian pleasure principle by rejecting free will, and it cannot be by accident that so many of the new brain scientists hold the same views regarding human nature at a time when we are seeing a counter-revolution against the social movements of the twentieth century.[21] Evolutionary psychology is simply the ideology that best suits the anti-social nature of Right-wing politics.[22]

While Dennett seems to be mostly blind to his own rhetoric and the social effects of his discourse, he does admit that evolutionary psychology has often been seen as an experiment in reverse engineering: "I cast evolutionary processes as design processes (processes of research and development, or R&D) and this adaptationist or reverse-engineering perspective has long lived under an undeserved cloud of suspicion" (22). The criticism he is anticipating here is the notion that evolutionary psychologists invent an unknowable past in order to justify how our current thoughts and actions are based on past solutions.[23] In other words, these scientists imagine what problems people faced hundreds of thousands of years ago, and then they claim that the solutions that were found in the distant past still shape our brains and minds through the process of natural selection.[24] To help to figure out what people in the past were actually thinking and doing, evolutionary psychologists look at fossils, current "primitive" cultures, primates, infants, and other clues. For instance, in trying to determine why we react so strongly to people we think are cheating society, evolutionary psychologists hypothesize that because hunter-gatherers must have had scare resources, they needed to make sure that everyone did their part to find food, and so all free-riders had to be punished.[25] We have therefore internalized a cheater detection program so that we automatically get upset at people we think are free-riding, and this is a source for our desire to punish "welfare cheats."[26] Through a process of reverse engineering, our political reactions to a current problem can therefore be traced back to the way our distant ancestors resolved their problems. Of course, this retroactive interpretative process leaves out history, culture, free will, rhetorical manipulation, and everything else that makes us human, yet isn't this reductionism one of its goals?

Dennett's discourse is not only reactionary, but it at times quite defensive in its desire to persuade its audience that they have no free will.[27] For instance, the following passage shows him trying to frame how his readers respond to his claims: "While I delight in having readers who are not only paying close attention but also way ahead of me, I would much prefer that you bide your time, cutting me some slack—giving me enough rope to hang myself, if you like—instead of trying to derail my attempt at a calm, objective account with your premonitions" (24). It is very interesting that as he is claiming that his argument is calm and objective, he is making an appeal for blind faith and the suspension of criticism. Here he appears to be asking his audience to eliminate their free will so that they can accept his argument that free will does not exist.

One of Dennett's calm and objective arguments is that there must be something in human nature that prevents women from being great thinkers:

> It is an obvious fact that although there have been many brilliant women of great attainment, none of them has achieved the iconic status of Aristotle, Bach, Copernicus, Dickens, Einstein ... I could easily list a dozen more men in the same league, but try for yourself to think of a great female thinker who could readily displace any of these men in playing the emblematic role in my title. (24)

Instead of blaming the lack of "great" women on prejudice, religion, ideology, discrimination, or oppression, Dennett has to stick with his investment in evolutionary psychology, and so this issue has to be blamed on biology and natural selection.[28] It is, of course, statements like this that often cause a lot of problems for evolutionary psychologists, who usually respond by claiming that they are only being objective and scientific, but what is really being displayed by this ignorance is a willful lack of care or concern for others.

One of Dennett's rhetorical strategies is to write something offensive, and then claim that it is not his view. In fact, it is often unclear what he is really trying to say because he takes opposed positions on the same point. For instance, in the following statement, he seeks to eliminate himself from the positions he has just articulated: "This polarization of visions, with cheering, hissing spectators egging on the combatants, is just a conveniently obvious first manifestation of the forces I am trying to render visible to all and neutralize" (25). He appears to be saying here that the offensive things he has written were only presented to get a strong reaction so that they could be then neutralized. In this ironic use of rhetoric, he is attempting to deny responsibility for his own words as he asks his audience to trust him that he knows what he is doing.

One of his strategies is to use mechanical metaphors and analogies in order to explain complex systems through simple representations.[29] However, the problem with this method is that in the effort to explain difficult ideas to an audience lacking the proper knowledge, important differences and ambiguities are repressed:

> Throughout this book I will exploit the perspective of reverse engineering, taking on the premise that every living thing is a product of nonmysterious physical processes that gradually brought all the elements together, refining them along the way, and eventually arrived at the working system we observe, or at some hypothesized intermediate system, a stepping-stone that would represent clear progress toward the living things we know exist. (28)

The paradox of this passage is that in his effort to provide the physical basis for all mental life, he ends up relying on a mental trick that breaks with reality. Thus, the human mind's ability to equate two different things (the mental and the physical) because they share something in common is one of the fundamental aspects of human consciousness transcending material reality, but Dennett wants to use this trick to deny that mental tricks happen in the first place.[30]

## The Return of the Death Drive

For Dennett, the guiding principle of all living entities is the need to store energy in order to replicate: "A living thing must capture enough energy and materials, and fend off its own destruction long enough to construct a good enough replica of itself" (29). This fundamental principle of genetic determinism is challenged by Freud's principle of the pleasure principle, which states that people receive enjoyment by escaping tension.[31] A key difference between these two principles is that Dennett's is about storing energy, while Freud's is based on releasing energy.[32] Thus, if Freud does have a biological theory, it is that unlike other living beings, we are not centered on storing energy or replicating. Instead, we are driven to eliminate stimulus, and this is why Freud is able to call the pleasure principle a death drive.[33] Ultimately, the goal of human life is the end of excitation and the purging of tension, which Aristotle called catharsis.[34]

We can see the evidence of the pleasure principle in our current culture's obsession with outsourcing all of our mental and physical activities to machines. It is as if we no longer want to spend any energy, and so we have built machines to do everything for us.[35] In fact, Freud argued that we are determined by a law of mental inertia, which means that we want to avoid all stimulation so that we can maintain a homeostatic level of energy.[36] By saying that the goal of life is death, Freud was implying that we are driven to be as lazy as possible while receiving the highest reward for the least amount of effort. It should be clear that this principle conflicts with natural selection and the competition for scarce reproductive resources. Moreover, it is only through our continual development of technological advances that we are better able to achieve the ultimate goal of the death drive. If the pleasure principle achieves its final goal, we will be able to download our consciousness into the cloud and sit back as we eliminate our ability to survive our own climate.[37] The greatest risk to humanity is thus the pleasure principle itself.

## Neo-animism

While Dennett does not consider the implications of Freud's theory, he does want to project a sense of purpose and design onto biological systems: "The biosphere is utterly saturated with design, with purpose, with reasons" (36). What may be going on in this attempt to locate a purpose in natural selection is a desire to deny human free will and then project it onto nature.[38] After all, evolution is supposed to work without a plan or intention since it is just the result of mutations, recombinations, and selective survival within a particular environment.[39] The reason why Dennett needs to inject intentionality into nature is that he wants to be able to draw an equivalence between humans and machines, and the mediating step to this process is to see nature as both mechanical and purposeful.

In this transference of human properties onto nonhuman entities, Dennett seeks to perversely show that while we humans lack free will and reason, we can find these human mental processes in nature itself: "The intentional stance works primarily for things that are designed to use information to accomplish their functions. It works by treating the thing as a rational agent, attributing 'beliefs' and 'desires' and 'rationality' to the thing, and predicting that it will act rationally" (37). We can call this type of claim neo-animism because it uses modern science to make an argument for the primitive belief in natural spirits.[40] In fact, Freud defined animism as the belief that there are no differences between our inner thoughts and the external world, and due to the magical belief in omnipotent thinking, reality can be changed through imagination.[41] Animism also implies that words are treated as things and things as words as the difference between memories and perceptions is effaced. One of the effects of this psychotic worldview is that human attributes are projected onto other animals and inanimate objects that are seen as having a spiritual existence.[42] For Freud, animism was the first form of civilization, and because inner thoughts were perceived as outer perceptions, there was no reality testing or scientific doubt.

In what I am calling neo-animism, we find the same projection of human mental processes onto other life forms and inanimate objects, but now this primitive process is rationalized through the use of the most developed technologies and scientific methodologies.[43] As a way of accomplishing the goals of the death drive and the pleasure principle, primary processes are employed so that magical thinking can be combined with scientific knowledge. Just as we seek to escape personal responsibility and social mediation by outsourcing our thinking and work to machines, we turn to pseudo-scientific theories to project our denied responsibility onto nonhuman beings and objects. By saying that the biosphere has purposes and reasons, we humanize nature as we dehumanize ourselves.[44]

One way that Dennett is able to both hold onto the blind process of natural selection and locate purpose in nature is by positing that nature blindly creates entities that have a purpose: "on the one hand they are blind, mindless, without goals, and on the other hand they produce designed entities galore, many of which become competent artificers" (37). Following the logic of Richard Dawkins, Dennett seeks to explain how a lack of purpose and design can turn into purposeful designing.[45] As a way of describing the leap from the physical to the mental and from the animal to the human, he has to rely on the paradoxical magic of turning a lack of purpose into a purposeful maker. Furthermore, in another example of neo-animism, the distinction between humans and machines has to be erased by seeing mechanical forces as spiritual entities.[46]

## The Meaning of Reason

Connected to the question of whether humans have free will, or are they just preprogrammed robots, is the issue of reason. Like many other evolutionary psychologists, Dennett tends to use the word reason to indicate two very different things. One definition of reason is found in the following passage:

> Wherever there are reasons, then, there is room for, and a need for, some kind of justification and the possibility of correction when something goes wrong. This "normativity" is the foundation of ethics: the ability to appreciate how reason-giving ought to go is a prerequisite for appreciating how life in society ought to go. Why and how did this practice and its rules arise? (41)

On one level, reason is represented here as embodying shared rules and norms, but on another level, reason simply means the ability to give an explanation for something.[47] Similar to the confusion between rationality and rationalizations, his use of the term *reason* can indicate any explanation or any social logic.[48] One of these definitions points to an explanation of something's purpose, and the other requires a distinction between the truth and a fiction. In fact, it is very hard to define reason itself because it has had so many different possible meanings.

According to Freud, what defines human reason is the ability to distinguish between our thoughts and our perceptions, and this distinction relies on suspending the pleasure principle in favor of the reality principle.[49] Freud adds that scientists use the reality principle by accepting the limits of knowledge and the inevitable necessities of nature.[50] However, instead of seeing reason as the human process of testing the reality of our knowledge and predictions, Dennett seeks to define reason as purpose, and then he projects purpose onto nature:

> Evolution by natural selection starts with how come and arrives at what for. We start with a lifeless world in which there are no reasons, no purposes at all, but there are processes that happen: rotating planets, tides, freezing, thawing, volcanic eruptions, and kazillions of chemical reactions. (40)

To show how even nature has a reason and a purpose, Dennett has to jump from how things function to why they do what they do.[51] This leap is made possible, in part, by using the word *reason* in two very different ways: one is functional, and the other is intentional, and because only humans have intentions, we can say that only humans have reasons, but these reasons are not in themselves reason.[52] Since reasons can be false and deceptive, they can go against our shared reason and objective understanding.

As Dennett indicates, our democratic legal system often relies on judging if someone is sane, and if they can apply reason in a rational way (41). However, the problem with this use of reason is that it once again confuses giving explanations with the testing of the reality of representations.[53] Moreover, once he confuses making an explanation with reason itself, he is able to project reason onto nature in another example of neo-animism. Thus, the only way we can say that nature has reasons is if we equate our thinking processes with non-human functions.

Since human reason relies on reality testing, Dennett has to argue that nature itself tests the reality of its own purposes:

> Natural selection is an algorithmic process, a collection of sorting algorithms that are themselves composed of generate-and-test algorithms that exploit randomness (pseudo-randomness, chaos) in the generation phase, and some sort of mindless quality-control testing phase, with the winners advancing in the tournament by having more offspring. (43)[54]

Here the mathematical concept of the algorithm is applied to natural processes, which are, in turn, equating with the testing of reality through trial-and-error experimentation.[55] In projecting math onto nature, human thought is once again confused with natural reality as science itself is represented as being part of natural selection.[56] However, what makes human reason human is precisely a break with nature through the use of abstraction, artificial logic, and symbolic generalization.[57] In an effort to treat humans as machines and machines as humans, neo-animism thus uses modern science to make very un-modern claims.

Through this book, I have been arguing that what makes us human is our break with nature, material reality, and evolution, and these three separations lead to a fourth divide, which is the ability of reason to go beyond the isolated individual through the formation of shared social institutions and practices.[58] While an individual can follow the reality principle and test reality in a scientific way, scientific reason is itself based on social consensus and critical introspection.[59] Just as analytic neutrality allows for free association to occur, learned impartiality enables reason to be applied without bias or a reliance on received authority.[60] In breaking with the pleasure principle, transference, and primary processes, human reason transcends our mental defense mechanisms, and yet Dennett wants to reverse this process by projecting reason back onto nature and machines.

## Fetishizing the Machine

As Marx argued, capitalism functions through the process of treating people like things and things like people, and this commodification of life is dependent on the type of neo-animism I have been discussing.[61] Freud adds that not only are we driven to release all tension to reach the death drive in the form of the pleasure principle, but this principle entails a drive to return to the inanimate.[62] We therefore want to see ourselves as objects so that we can escape from any responsibility or tension, and this drive towards death is evident in the way that we have become so attached to our technologies that we would rather spend time with them than interacting with people in a live setting.[63] The drive then to see the human mind as a computer has the reverse effect of seeing computers as human beings. Neo-animism thus fuels Neoliberalism as people seek to replace social regulation with automated systems and bottom-up markets, which take on a life of their own.[64] In turn, evolutionary psychology is an ideological tool helping to provide a scientific explanation for an anti-scientific mythology.[65]

These issues are so important because the biggest threat to humankind may be the way we rely on our technologies to provide instant pleasure through an escape from reality and responsibility.[66] One reason, then, why we may do nothing to fight climate change or to stop pandemics is that we are so enthralled by our media devices that we no longer really value nature, life, or reality. By seeing the pleasure principle as a death drive, we can try to reverse this process, which also requires fighting against the temptation of neo-animism.[67]

## Notes

1　Dennett, Daniel C. From bacteria to Bach and back: The evolution of minds. WW Norton & Company, 2017.

2　Maung, Hane Htut. "Daniel C. Dennett: From Bacteria to Bach and Back. The Evolution of Minds." Synthesis philosophica35.1 (2020): 267–270.

3　Hofstadter, Douglas R. I am a strange loop. Basic books, 2007.

4　Lindeman, David. "Daniel Dennett," From Bacteria to Bach and Back: The Evolution of Minds." Reviewed by." Philosophy in Review 38.2 (2018): 55–57.

5　Samuels, Robert. "Damasio's Error: The Politics of Biological Determinism After Freud." Psychoanalyzing the Politics of the New Brain Sciences. Palgrave Pivot, Cham, 2017. 9–33.

6　Descartes, René, and Donald A. Cress. Discourse on method. Hackett Publishing, 1998.

7　Davis, Philip J., and Reuben Hersh. Descartes' dream: The world according to mathematics. Courier Corporation, 2005.

8　Diamond, Marie Josephine. "The social configuration of Descartes' Discourse on Method." Dialectical Anthropology 7.1 (1982): 1–9.

9　Baker, Gordon P., Gordon Baker, and Katherine J. Morris. Descartes' dualism. Psychology Press, 2002.

10　Dave, Malay, and Vidya Giri Shankar. "from bacteria to bach and back: The evolution of minds–Daniel Dennett." Annals of Indian Psychiatry 2.1 (2018): 70.

11　Lindeman, David. "Daniel Dennett," From Bacteria to Bach and Back: The Evolution of Minds." Reviewed by." Philosophy in Review 38.2 (2018): 55–57.

12　Żywiczyński, Przemysław. "Biological Evolution, Cultural Evolution and the Evolution of Language. Review of Daniel Dennett's From Bacteria to Bach and Back." Theoria et Historia Scientiarum 16 (2019): 169.

13　Miller, Jacques-Alain, ed. The Seminar of Jacques Lacan: Book 1: Freud's Papers on Technique 1953–1954. CUP Archive, 1988.

14　Samuels, Robert. "Ethos, Transference, and Liberal Cynicism." Zizek and the Rhetorical Unconscious. Palgrave Macmillan, Cham, 2020. 49–63.

15　Samuels, Robert. "Catharsis: The Politics of Enjoyment." Zizek and the Rhetorical Unconscious. Palgrave Macmillan, Cham, 2020. 7–31.

16　Butler, Eamonn. Friedrich Hayek: The ideas and influence of the libertarian economist. Harriman House Limited, 2012.

17　Samuels, Robert. "Auto-modernity after postmodernism: Autonomy and auto-mation in culture, technology, and education." Digital youth, innovation, and the unexpected (2008).

18　Skott-Myhre, Hans. "Marx, ideology, and the unconscious." Annual Review of Critical Psychology 12 (2015): 59–65.

19　Double, Richard. "The moral hardness of libertarianism." Philo5.2 (2002): 226–234.

20　Freud, Sigmund. "Formulations on the two principles of mental functioning." The Standard Edition of the Complete Psychological Works of Sigmund Freud, Volume XII (1911–1913): The Case of Schreber, Papers on Technique and Other Works. 1958. 213–226.

21　Samuels, Robert. "The Brain Sciences Against the Welfare State." Psychoanalyzing the Politics of the New Brain Sciences. Palgrave Pivot, Cham, 2017. 85–114.

22　Kendall, Gavin. "From liberalism to neoliberalism." Social Change in the twenty-first century 2003 Conference Refereed Proceedings. Centre for Social Change Research, School of Humanities and Human Services QUT, 2003.

23 Buller, David J. "Evolutionary psychology: the emperor's new paradigm." Trends in cognitive sciences 9.6 (2005): 277–283.
24 Richardson, Robert C. Evolutionary psychology as maladapted psychology. MIT press, 2010.
25 Petersen, Michael Bang, et al. "Who deserves help? Evolutionary psychology, social emotions, and public opinion about welfare." Political psychology 33.3 (2012): 395–418.
26 Petersen, Michael Bang. "Social welfare as small-scale help: evolutionary psychology and the deservingness heuristic." American Journal of Political Science 56.1 (2012): 1–16.
27 Baer, John, James C. Kaufman, and Roy F. Baumeister, eds. Are we free? Psychology and free will. Oxford University Press, 2008.
28 Ruti, Mari. The age of scientific sexism: How evolutionary psychology promotes gender profiling and fans the battle of the sexes. Bloomsbury Publishing USA, 2015.
29 Gantt, Edwin E., Brent S. Melling, and Jeffrey S. Reber. "Mechanisms or metaphors? The emptiness of evolutionary psychological explanations." Theory & Psychology 22.6 (2012): 823–841.
30 Smith, L. "Metaphors of knowledge and behaviour." Metaphors in the history of psychology (1990): 239–267.
31 Samuels, Robert. "Catharsis: The Politics of Enjoyment." Zizek and the Rhetorical Unconscious. Palgrave Macmillan, Cham, 2020. 7–31.
32 Freud, Sigmund. "Project for a scientific psychology (1950 [1895])." The Standard Edition of the Complete Psychological Works of Sigmund Freud, Volume I (1886–1899): Pre-Psycho-Analytic Publications and Unpublished Drafts. 1966. 281–391.
33 Freud, Sigmund. Beyond the pleasure principle. Penguin UK, 2003.
34 Butcher, Samuel Henry, ed. The poetics of Aristotle. Macmillan, 1907.
35 Leonhard, Gerd. Technology vs. Humanity: The coming clash between man and machine. FutureScapes, 2016.
36 Foxe, Arthur, N. "Critique of Freud's concept of a death instinct." Psychoanalytic Review 30.4 (1943): 417–427.
37 Ruti, Mari. "The singularity of being: Lacan and the immortal within." Journal of the American Psychoanalytic Association58.6 (2010): 1113–1138.
38 Nanay, Bence. "Symmetry between the intentionality of minds and machines? The biological plausibility of Dennett's account." Minds and Machines 16.1 (2006): 57–71.
39 Dawkins, Richard. The selfish gene. Oxford university press, 2016.
40 Richardson, Kathleen. "Technological animism: The uncanny personhood of humanoid machines." Social Analysis 60.1 (2016): 110–128.
41 Freud, Sigmund. "Animism, magic and the omnipotence of thoughts." Totem and Taboo (1913): 75–99.
42 Guthrie, Stewart. "Animal animism: Evolutionary roots of religious cognition." Current approaches in the cognitive science of religion (2002): 38–67.
43 Taylor, Bron. "Dark Green Religion: Gaian Earth Spirituality, Neo-Animism, and the Transformation of Global Environmental Politics." Annual Meeting of the American Academy of Religion. 2007.
44 Norenzayan, Ara, Ian G. Hansen, and Jasmine Cady. "An angry volcano? Reminders of death and anthropomorphizing nature." Social Cognition 26.2 (2008): 190–197.
45 Dawkins, Richard. "Darwinism and human purpose." Human origins (1989): 137–143.

46 Caporael, Linnda R. "Anthropomorphism and mechanomorphism: Two faces of the human machine." Computers in human behavior 2.3 (1986): 215–234.
47 Stich, Stephen P. "Dennett on intentional systems." Philosophical Topics 12.1 (1981): 39–62.
48 Samuels, Robert. "Damasio's Error: The Politics of Biological Determinism After Freud." Psychoanalyzing the Politics of the New Brain Sciences. Palgrave Pivot, Cham, 2017. 9–33.
49 Freud, Sigmund. "Formulations on the two principles of mental functioning." The Standard Edition of the Complete Psychological Works of Sigmund Freud, Volume XII (1911–1913): The Case of Schreber, Papers on Technique and Other Works. 1958. 213–226.
50 Samuels, Robert. "Science and the Reality Principle." Freud for the Twenty-First Century. Palgrave Pivot, Cham, 2019. 5–16.
51 Zahavi, Dan. "Killing the straw man: Dennett and phenomenology." Phenomenology and the cognitive sciences6.1-2 (2007): 21–43.
52 Spence, Sean. "Descartes' error: Emotion, reason and the human brain." BMJ 310.6988 (1995): 1213.
53 Peczenik, Aleksander. On law and reason. Vol. 8. Springer Science & Business Media, 2008.
54 Dennett, Daniel C., and Daniel Clement Dennett. Darwin's Dangerous Idea: Evolution and the Meanins of Life. No. 39. Simon and Schuster, 1996.
55 Swenson, Rod. "Evolutionary theory developing: The problem (s) with Darwin's dangerous idea." Ecological Psychology 9.1 (1997): 47–96.
56 Orr, H. Allen. "Dennett's strange idea." Boston Review 21.3 (1996).
57 Osborne, Peter. "The reproach of abstraction." Radical Philosophy 127 (2004): 21–28.
58 Tuomela, Raimo. "Collective acceptance, social institutions, and social reality." American Journal of Economics and Sociology 62.1 (2003): 123–165.
59 Lehrer, Keith, and Carl Wagner. Rational consensus in science and society: A philosophical and mathematical study. Vol. 24. Springer Science & Business Media, 2012.
60 Gerson, Samuel. "Neutrality, resistance, and self-disclosure in an intersubjective psychoanalysis." Psychoanalytic Dialogues6.5 (1996): 623–645.
61 Billig, Michael. "Commodity fetishism and repression: Reflections on Marx, Freud and the psychology of consumer capitalism." Theory & Psychology 9.3 (1999): 313–329.
62 Freud, Sigmund. Beyond the pleasure principle. Penguin UK, 2003.
63 Jhally, Sut. The codes of advertising: Fetishism and the political economy of meaning in the consumer society. Routledge, 2014.
64 Hooley, Tristram. "A war against the robots? Career guidance, automation and neoliberalism." Career guidance for social justice: Contesting neoliberalism (2018): 93–108.
65 Samuels, Robert. Psychoanalyzing the Politics of the New Brain Sciences. Springer, 2017.
66 Baudrillard, Jean. "The ecstasy of communication, trans." B. Schutze and C. Schutze, New York: Semiotext (e) (1988).
67 Samuels, Robert. "Conclusion: Communism or Commonism?." Zizek and the Rhetorical Unconscious. Palgrave Macmillan, Cham, 2020. 87–92.

# Chapter 6

# Psychoanalysis Beyond Machines and Animals

Throughout this book, I have argued that we need psychoanalysis to fully understand what makes us human; however, as I will discuss throughout this chapter, this application of psychoanalytic thought is hindered by how easy it is to misunderstand its fundamental concepts and practices. For instance, a central problem has been that Freud used common words to point to very uncommon ideas. Thus, when Freud and other psychoanalysts talk about consciousness or sexuality, they often mean something very different from what most people think. Since psychoanalysis argues that our minds transcend material reality and our words often say more than we want or less than we desire, it is hard for psychoanalysts to talk about psychoanalysis. Therefore, while I have been arguing that psychoanalysis helps us to understand what makes us human, this comprehension has been undermined by the misunderstanding of psychoanalysis itself. In fact, as I will show in this chapter, many psychoanalysts are now turning to neuroscience and evolutionary psychology to make Freud's work more scientific, but the end result is the total repression of analysis.

## Misunderstanding Psychoanalytic Practice

What is most often not understood about psychoanalytic practice is that the analyst has to refrain from responding to the patient's fundamental demand for love, recognition, and knowledge.[1] In other words, the analyst should not feed the transference by becoming a source of understanding, care, or judgment.[2] Not only, then, is psychoanalysis not a "natural" way of interacting with other people, but also it requires a great deal of self-restraint and confidence in the process. Likewise, it is very difficult for people to learn how to free associate since they are so used to thinking about what other people are thinking about them.[3] Yet, it is the neutrality of the analyst that allows for the free association of the patent, and virtually all of psychoanalytic practice is dependent on keeping free association going.[4] Unfortunately, many analysts, therapists, and psychiatrists

DOI: 10.4324/9781003364610-6

have given up on neutrality and free association, and so we can see that psychoanalysis is being repressed within psychoanalysis.

One reason why analytic neutrality is so important to the issue of determining what makes us human is that this suspension of bias defines the foundation of modern science and democratic law.[5] As a purely human invention, neutrality makes reason possible as it opens up the thinking person to the ability to test reality from an objective and impartial perspective. Just as Descartes posited that the scientist must suspend all biases and prejudices in order to apply logic to empirical reality, human beings have to learn how to move beyond the pleasure principle and their dependency on others as they accept the limitations of their own knowledge.[6] In other terms, part of being human is the ability to work through transference, fantasy, and magical thinking. From this perspective, there is something anti-human about being human since the very things that make us different from other animals and machines have to also be transcended.

Currently, many analysts reject the possibility of analytic neutrality because they think that it comes off as too cold and distant.[7] They also do not want to let their patients suffer in silence, and they enjoy being a source of knowledge, identification, and reality testing. In fact, many therapists feel that it is their job to provide signs of empathy, and to do this, they must understand what their patients are saying and feeling.[8] Yet, part of the working through of the transference entails the recognition that people never do completely understand each other, and that we often impose our own thoughts and feelings onto others. Since psychoanalysis is about discovering something new, it cannot be based on the already known. Furthermore, Freud realized that if an understanding came from the analyst, the patient would most likely not take it to heart because one has to learn things for oneself in order for them to be taken seriously.[9] Since conviction comes from personal experience, the analyst has to give up on being the source of knowledge and interpretation for the patient. Like the Zen master who refuses to be a master, the analyst has to help the patient to not rely on the knowledge, love, and recognition of others.[10]

Many psychoanalysts do not see how human freedom is in part based on breaking with transferring responsibility onto others, and so they do not help their patients become independent.[11] Just as parents have a hard time watching their children fail or suffer, therapists want to come to the rescue, and they often take on the role of being a friend, an educator, a parent, or an advisor, but Freud warned against the analyst taking on all of these positions.[12] In fact, the only way to discover what we want from others is if others do not give us what we want. The analyst has to thus refuse to respond to the demands of the patient so that the driving force behind these demands becomes evident.[13]

## Neuro-Psychoanalysis?

The repression of psychoanalysis is also evident in the recent efforts to develop a combination of neuroscience and psychoanalysis. In looking at Mark Solms' *The Feeling Brain*, we can examine how this attempted reconciliation often results in repressing what makes us human by returning to pre-Freudian notions of instincts, consciousness, the unconscious, and transference.[14] Not only does neuro-psychoanalysis block us from understanding our humanity but it also functions to feed the replacement of analysis with a pseudo-techno-science.

Like the works of Harris, Pinker, and Dennett, we find at times in Solms a self-reflexive awareness of how his own discourse will be received: "What it really means is psychoanalysis minus the psyche, psychoanalysis biologized and reduced to neuroscience, with psychoanalysis being eliminated in the process" (1). In this quote, we find Solms' representing the truth of his own discourse, which is bent on applying biological determinism to psychoanalysis. Perhaps, we can read this admission as a return of the repressed where Solms cannot help but admit that his work threatens to remove subjectivity from psychoanalysis.

In Solms' case, we can see how his desire to prove psychoanalytic theories and concepts through an empirical method forces him to repress the truth of psychoanalytic practice:

> The laws governing the development and functions of the human personality must surely, somehow be reconcilable with the laws governing these aspects of the human brain; since who can deny that the brain is the organ of the mind—that these two things (mind and brain) are ultimately the same part of nature. (1)

By equating the brain and the mind, Solms seeks to place psychoanalysis on firmer ground since it can now be treated as any other natural science, and thus the social legitimacy of the hard science can become associated with analysis.[15] However, as we have seen in previous chapters, this conflation of the mind and the brain represents one of the central ways that psychoanalysis is itself repressed. Since a defining aspect of what makes us human is the ability of our minds to transcend our brains, our break with reality means that we cannot understand psychoanalysis or ourselves by returning to the natural sciences.

Solms not only desires to conceal the distinction between the mind and the brain but also wants to return to a biological model of human subjectivity: "Freud's great contribution sprang from his recognition that mental life is unavoidably tethered to the body, and thereby to biology. There can be no mind without body" (3). Although Freud did often concentrate on the relation between the mind and the body, his theory of drives and the pleasure principle represent a radical break with biology and the other natural sciences.[16] Since we seek to avoid tension by accessing pleasure, anything can be a source of enjoyment, and this means that humans are not determined by inherited instincts.[17] Furthermore, I have posited that one of the roots of our free will, which leads to mental autonomy, is the fact of our lack of biological determinism, which also entails that we cannot use evolution to understand what it means to be human.

In contrast to Freud's break with biology and evolution, Solms returns to this pre-Freudian understanding of human instincts: "In fact, according to Freud, the very existence of the mind—of a sentient instrument for learning how to meet our vital and reproductive needs in the world—is a product of evolutionary biological forces" (3). Actually, Freud ended up arguing the exact opposite of what Solms is affirming: humans are not driven primarily by need for reproduction because human sexuality is polymorphous and perverse and transcends its organic foundation.[18] While it is true that there is a biological and natural aspect to our drives, what makes these forces human is their openness and variability.[19] However, like many evolutionary psychologists, Solms insists that our subjectivity is defined by evolution: "The mind is not exempt from the laws of natural selection" (3). We shall see that this desire to base psychoanalysis on evolution functions to repress psychoanalysis itself as it denies what makes us human.

Of course, one of the most direct ways to deny the human is to equate people with other animals. Even though, we know that these animals do not have free will, consciousness, language, or reason, we often experiment on these beings in order to discover things about ourselves: "Affective neuroscience is based mainly in animal research, in which the emotional effects of various experimental manipulations (ablations, electrical stimulations, etc.) are systematically observed in order to discern the basic affective circuitry of the mammalian brain. Since such circuits are so fundamental (with emotion being such a basic brain function), they are conserved in human beings" (6). It should be evident that our emotions are very different from the affective states of other animals, but because Solms equates minds and brains and endorses evolutionary psychology, he desires to legitimate animal research as a way of discovering human attributes. As Lacan argued, experiments on animals are a form of neo-animism because they are often based on the projection of human thought processes onto these creatures.[20] Since other animals do not have guilt or shame, they are fundamentally different from us, and to repress this difference is to obscure what makes us human.

Of course, people doing pharmacological research have a hard time experimenting directly with humans, and so they turn to other animals as a way of tracking the ways different chemicals affect these animals, but even when they find a correlation between a chemical and response, they do not gain much insight into why humans respond in a certain way. Yet, Solms calls for psychoanalysis to turn to animals because he thinks this type of research will help to place analysis on firmer ground.[21] Moreover, he believes that Freud would have done the same thing if he lived today and had all of the same technology: "Throughout his later psychoanalytic work he had a specific scientific programme in mind, largely continuous with his earlier neuroscientific work, albeit shaped by the limitations of the scientific methods and techniques available to him at that time" (14). This common notion that Freud was just born too early to understand what makes us human is based on a complete rejection of what makes psychoanalysis a special discourse: it is the break with nature and biology, which helps to clear a space for psychoanalytic thinking.[22]

Instead of recognizing what makes humans different from other animals, Solms is bent on applying a reductive evolutionary model to the human mind: "It is unquestionably significant that evolutionary selective pressures advantage organisms that develop better—that is, more accurate—models of reality. In a world without vision, the first animals to evolve organs of sight would be highly advantaged" (20). However, due to our break with nature and our mental autonomy, we are not driven to develop more accurate models of reality; instead, we often engage in self-deception, misrepresentation, and the denial of reality. If we were simply determined by the quest to be shaped by more accurate models of reality, then psychoanalysis would not have to exist. As Freud first discovered in his encounter with hysterics, their symptoms did not make anatomical or cognitive sense, and due to the pleasure principle, they often sought to escape reality through the processes of repression, substitution, displacement, and conversion.[23] It is thus simply absurd to say that we are shaped by an evolutionary drive to have an accurate picture of the world. Perhaps, this drive for truer representations is the desire of the scientist, but it does not shape much of human thinking or experience.

To close the gap between the human and other animals, Solms turns to technology to create a strict equivalence between brain structures and mental processes: "Moreover, by virtue of advances in structural imaging, it is possible to identify the neural basis of the clinically observed phenomena in neurological patients with a high level of scientific accuracy—a method well-suited for establishing clinical-anatomical correlations" (23). This type of anatomical localization has come under much criticism, and yet Solms wants to use this method in order to make psychoanalysis more scientific, but the cost is the repression of the psychoanalytic understanding of what makes us human.[24] Since we have the ability to manipulate our bodily sensations and turn pain into pleasure, neurotic symptoms reveal that break with anatomy and biological determinism.

While what happens in our minds often has an effect on what happens in our brains, it is important not to see a one-to-one correspondence between the two. For instance, just because a particular brain injury causes one to lose a specific mental function that does not mean that the mental process is created by a particular organic structure.[25] After all, if a piano key breaks, and you can no longer play Mozart, it does not mean that Mozart's music was a direct reflection of the piano's parts. Still, Solms constantly represses this distinction between the mind and the brain so that he can use neuroscientific findings to make psychoanalysis more acceptable to others:

> In Kaplan-Solms and Solms (2000) we describe psychoanalytic obser-
> vations on a small series of patients with right parietal lesions. They
> exhibited a remarkable degree of self-deception, in that they were
> paralysed (on the left side) but insisted that they were not paralysed. (27)

Although damage to a particular region of the brain may prevent certain mental processes that does not mean that we can explain our mental states by determining what brain region has been affected.[26] Clearly broken hardware can prevent the software from functioning properly, but this does not mean that understanding the hardware will tell us how the software has been designed.

In an effort to find a biological cause for every mental problem, Solms follows other neuroscientists and evolutionary psychologists by offering a reductive understanding of the human mind: "Kaplan-Solms and Solms (2000) concluded that self-deception in right parietal lobe damage might well be attributable to narcissistic defensive organizations, such that the patients avoided depressive affects, using a range of primitive defence mechanisms" (27). I have argued elsewhere that the intentional or unintentional effect of this type of argument is to position drugs as the only possible treatment for mental issues.[27] Since we cannot simply replace damaged parts of the brain yet, we have to find a way to re-wire the brain through the manipulation of neurotransmitters. However, what is missed by this approach is not only the human break with biology and materiality but also what is repressed is the way purely mental processes can have a direct effect on brain structures and the release or blocking of particular neurotransmitters.[28] From this perspective, there is a relationship between the mind and the brain, but the relationship is dialectical and not simply from the brain to the mind.

Instead of accepting this dialectical structure, Solms constantly returns to the desire to base the mind on the evolved biology of the brain: "psycho-analytic observations on how the mind is altered by damage to different parts of the brain has enabled us to begin to build up a coherent model of how the mental apparatus, as we understand it in psychoanalysis, is realized in anatomy and physiology" (29). Perhaps this effort to center psycho-analysis on brain research will increase the acceptance of analysis, but the price will be the sacrifice of psychoanalysis itself, which also entails a lost ability for us to understand what makes us human.

## The Human Sciences

Solms' work forces us to ask what defines science itself and is psychoanalysis a science?[29] Although I do believe that we can base psychoanalytic theory on an objective analysis of mental material, this does not mean that we need to rely on the natural sciences to explain the human mind. In fact, I have been arguing that neuroscience and evolutionary psychology are themselves often not real sciences because they rely on a series of false equivalences that block their desire for a more accurate picture of reality.[30] By equating the mind with the brain and the human with other animals, we do not gain a better understanding of ourselves; instead, this turn to the natural sciences only functions to replace empiricism with ideology through the development of a new form of animism. We see this desire to locate human mental processes in nature in the following passage: "The mind, is, after all, just a part of nature—it must somehow be reducible to lawful mechanisms that can be precisely defined in objective, third-person terms" (36). What I think Solms is really doing here is manipulating language to persuade his audience to see psychoanalysis as just as legitimate as the natural sciences. He is not really providing a more accurate picture of what makes us human: he is engaging in a rhetorical process to attain social status. Moreover, psychoanalytic practice is not based on third-party observations since it is only the words of the patient that matter. Therefore, when one translates these words into meaningful interpretations, one is moving from practice to theory, and this requires certain distortions and revisions.[31]

Since we have to differentiate the practice of psychoanalysis from its theory, it is important to first understand why we need a theory in the first place. I believe that one of the main reasons for Freud's development of meta-psychology was that he had to convince analysts that they should not act like other doctors or spiritual advisors.[32] The theory then helps to shape the practice by clearing the space for a different way of acting. Since it is not natural to be neutral or to free associate, these artificial practices have to be rationalized and justified from within the theory itself. It is also necessary to make certain diagnostic judgments so that one does not treat psychotic patients in the same way as one would treat neurotics. Since you do not want to push psychotics to go into full regression in treatment, it is essential to determine if a patient is psychotic or not.[33] In order to make this determination, one needs a theory of psychosis related to other psychopathologies. We can therefore consider Freud's theoretical system as built from the necessity of treating people in a psychoanalytic way. Freud would also apply his understanding of unconscious processes to different social and cultural phenomenon, but this type of application was itself grounded in the knowledge gained from the practice of analysis itself.

Since analysts like Solms seem to have very little understanding of what psychoanalytic treatment actually entails, it is easy for them to turn to other disciplines in order to understand analysis. Moreover, one reason why Solms feels that psychoanalysis cannot explain or legitimate itself is that he sees consciousness and subjectivity as inaccessible to scientific observation: "Consciousness cannot be observed externally; it is not amenable to objective scrutiny. Consciousness is for that reason an embarrassment to science, the ideal of which is objective fact over subjective experience" (40). What Solms refuses to accept is the basic Freudian idea that we can directly observe and analyze subjective states since these states are themselves structured through language and other types of symbolic representations. If we think of symbols as the atoms of human consciousness, then we can study directly this material in a scientific way.[34] We can also use our knowledge of unconscious processes to predict how people will act, and we do not need brain scans to make these predictions.

By misunderstanding the essence of consciousness, Solms mystifies psychoanalysis and ends up legitimating neuroscience and evolutionary psychology: "It is, in my view, no accident that the apparent re-admittance of consciousness to psychology coincided with advances in the neurosciences which made it possible to study the physiological correlates of almost any mental state" (97). In this high-tech form of magical thinking, human mental processes are equated with physical structures, which then further removes us from understanding consciousness.[35] This neo-animism is an actual example of what it is refusing to understand: since human thought goes beyond material reality, pseudo-science can imagine things that do not actually exist.

Although, Solms does at times try to move beyond biological determinism, he cannot help but return to this discourse in order to ground his arguments in more acceptable theories: "This brain system evolved from general pain mechanisms more than 200 million years ago, apparently for the purpose of forging long-term attachments between mothers and their offspring, between sexual mates, and ultimately between social groups in general" (113). This use of evolutionary psychology to explain human feelings simply discounts mental autonomy and the openness of human drives, which are shaped by culture and personal experience.[36] While psychoanalysis does not deny that nature and evolution play some role in human consciousness, they cannot be the sole source for subjectivity.

## Drugging Analysis

We know that one reason why psychiatrists, psychoanalysts, and psychologists have turned to biological models of the mind was the desire to receive more funding and social recognition.[37] By seeing mental disorders as diseases, not only could these professionals make their discourses appear more scientific, but they also could clear a path for a closer relationship with the lucrative pharmaceutical industry.[38] Furthermore, since federal funding was available for the testing of medication and medical theories of mental diseases, researchers were motivated to turn to a biological model.[39] The end result of this collusion among psychologists, pharmacologists, universities, and government agencies can be found in the following passage:

> This system is embodied in a well-defined network of brain structures ... Activation and deactivation of this system is fundamentally mediated by opioid receptors. Mu-opioid agonists in particular activate it in such a way as to generate feelings of secure well-being that are the very opposite of depression, whereas mu-opioid blockade or withdrawal produces separation distress. This state is most readily identified in animal models by distress vocalizations. (103–104)

In the treatment of depression with opiates, we not only see some of the roots of the opiate epidemic, but we also witness the danger of explaining psychological states through neuro-anatomy and bio-chemistry: by eliminating what makes is human, we become programmable machines that can be manipulated through medication.[40] There is clearly little room for talk therapy or psychoanalysis in this discourse, and yet, Solms wants to combine neuroscience with psychoanalysis.

Since Solms also does not understand the radical nature of Freud's theories of sexuality and the pleasure principle, he is able to argue that psychoanalysis has had little to tell us about addiction. (109). The truth of the matter is that Freud helps us to understand addiction better than any other model because only Freud fully articulates the connection between pleasure and escape.[41] Not only can humans sexualize any object, including their own thoughts and bodies, but sexualization enables a replacement of suffering with pleasure as one escape tension and conflict and ultimately reality.[42] This theory of addiction is spread throughout Freud's work, and so Solms simply does not understand what a non-biological model of compulsive behavior means.

Lacan was fond of saying that if we want to understand science, we have to understand the desire of the scientist.[43] In Solms' case, it is clear that his desire to combine psychoanalysis and neuroscience is driven by a need to pursue the truth of what makes us human while also seeking to gain social acceptance for his discourse. Since these two desires are in conflict with each other, he can only split his rhetoric and jump from one perspective to the other without confronting what happens when the two views confront each other.[44] It has been my argument that there can be no compromise in psychoanalytic theory and practice because the uniqueness of this approach makes it the best suited to help us understand what makes us human.

One reason why we need to answer this question of our humanness is revealed in Solms' discussion of addiction. Since pleasure plays such a huge role in issues like substance abuse, virtual reality consumption, and libertarian politics, we have to see how human pleasure is different from other animals.[45] By connecting pleasure to escape, we can comprehend how we are driven to avoid tension, guilt, and shame, and this death drive could result in not only our own self-destruction but the destruction of our planet. There is simply no way to fight climate change, global pandemics, dire poverty, or lethal drug addictions, if we do not exchange our easy access to pleasure for a direct confrontation with reality.[46] This means not only accepting the truth of the world around us but also accepting our own truth. Since, as Freud insisted, we cannot erase our own memories, we have no choice but to investigate ourselves in an open and honest way.

## Notes

1 Nobus, Dany. Jacques Lacan and the Freudian practice of psychoanalysis. Psychology Press, 2000.
2 Fink, Bruce. "Against understanding: Why understanding should not be viewed as an essential aim of psychoanalytic treatment." Journal of the American Psychoanalytic Association 58.2 (2010): 259–285.
3 Freud, Sigmund. "Notes upon a case of obsessional neurosis." The Standard Edition of the Complete Psychological Works of Sigmund Freud, Volume X (1909): Two Case Histories ('Little Hans' and the 'Rat Man'). 1955. 151–318.
4 Freud, Sigmund. "The dynamics of transference." The standard edition of the complete psychological works of Sigmund Freud, Volume XII (1911–1913): The case of Schreber, papers on technique and other works. 1958. 97–108.
5 Samuels, Robert. "Science and the Reality Principle." Freud for the Twenty-First Century. Palgrave Pivot, Cham, 2019. 5–16.
6 Descartes, René, and Donald A. Cress. Discourse on method. Hackett Publishing, 1998.
7 Chodorow, Nancy J. Feminism and psychoanalytic theory. Yale University Press, 1989.
8 Kohut, Heinz. "Introspection, empathy, and psychoanalysis an examination of the relationship between mode of observation and theory." Journal of the American psychoanalytic association 7.3 (1959): 459–483.
9 Rieff, Philip. Freud: The mind of the moralist. University of Chicago Press, 1979.
10 Moncayo, Raul. "The finger pointing at the moon: Zen practice and the practice of Lacanian psychoanalysis." Psychoanalysis and Buddhism: An unfolding dialogue (2003): 331–386.
11 Benjamin, Jessica. The Bonds of Love: Psychoanalysis, Feminism, and the Problem of Domincation. Pantheon, 2013.
12 Freud, Sigmund. The question of lay analysis: Conversations with an impartial person. WW Norton & Company, 1969.
13 Terman, David. "Optimum frustration: Structuralization and the therapeutic process." Learning from Kohut: Progr. Self Psychol4 (1988): 113–26.
14 Solms, Mark. The feeling brain: Selected papers on neuropsychoanalysis. Routledge, 2018.
15 Bowlby, John. "Psychoanalysis as a natural science." International Review of Psycho-Analysis 8 (1981): 243–256.
16 Freud, Sigmund. Beyond the pleasure principle. Penguin UK, 2003.

17 Lacan, Jacques. "The ethics of psychoanalysis: The seminar of Jacques Lacan: Book VII." (2015).
18 Freud, Sigmund. Three essays on the theory of sexuality: The 1905 edition. Verso Books, 2017.
19 Freud, Sigmund. "Instincts and their vicissitudes." The Standard Edition of the Complete Psychological Works of Sigmund Freud, Volume XIV (1914–1916): On the History of the Psycho-Analytic Movement, Papers on Metapsychology and Other Works. 1957. 109–140.
20 Lacan, Jacques. The four fundamental concepts of psycho-analysis. Vol. 11. WW Norton & Company, 1998.
21 Kirkwood, James K. "The distribution of the capacity for sentience in the animal kingdom." Animals, Ethics and Trade. Routledge, 2012. 38–52.
22 Laurent, Eric. "Uses of neurosciences for psychoanalysis." La Cause Freudienn 70 (2008).
23 Breuer, Josef, and Sigmund Freud. Studies on hysteria. Hachette UK, 2009.
24 Catani, Marco, et al. "Beyond cortical localization in clinico-anatomical correlation." cortex 48.10 (2012): 1262–1287.
25 Zola-Morgan, Stuart. "Localization of brain function: The legacy of Franz Joseph Gall (1758–1828)." Annual review of neuroscience 18.1 (1995): 359–383.
26 Young, Robert Maxwell. Mind, brain, and adaptation in the nineteenth century: cerebral localization and its biological context from Gall to Ferrier. No. 3. Oxford University Press, USA, 1990.
27 Samuels, Robert. "Drugging Discontent: Psychoanalysis, Drives, and the Governmental University Medical Pharmaceutical Complex (GUMP)." Psychoanalyzing the Politics of the New Brain Sciences. Palgrave Pivot, Cham, 2017. 115–136.
28 Engel, George L., and Arthur H. Schmale Jr. "Psychoanalytic theory of somatic disorder conversion, specificity, and the disease onset situation." Journal of the American Psychoanalytic Association 15.2 (1967): 344–365.
29 Glynos, Jason, and Yannis Stavrakakis, eds. Lacan and science. Routledge, 2018.
30 Samuels, Robert. Psychoanalyzing the Politics of the New Brain Sciences. Springer, 2017.
31 Freud, Sigmund. "A note on the unconscious in psycho-analysis." The Standard Edition of the Complete Psychological Works of Sigmund Freud, Volume XII (1911–1913): The Case of Schreber, Papers on Technique and Other Works. 1958. 255–266.
32 Freud, Sigmund. The question of lay analysis: Conversations with an impartial person. WW Norton & Company, 1969.
33 Fink, Bruce. A clinical introduction to Lacanian psychoanalysis: Theory and technique. Harvard University Press, 2009.
34 De Maat, Saskia, et al. "The current state of the empirical evidence for psychoanalysis: a meta-analytic approach." Harvard review of psychiatry 21.3 (2013): 107–137.
35 Legrenzi, Paolo, and Carlo Umiltà. Neuromania: On the limits of brain science. Oxford University Press, 2011.
36 Rose, Hilary, and Steven Rose. Alas poor Darwin: Arguments against evolutionary psychology. Random House, 2010.
37 Whitaker, Robert. "Anatomy of an epidemic: Psychiatric drugs and the astonishing rise of mental illness in America." Ethical Human Psychology and Psychiatry 7.1 (2005): 23.

38 Moncrieff, Joanna. "The myth of the chemical cure." The Myth of the Chemical Cure. Palgrave Macmillan, London, 2008. 217–224.
39 Kirsch, Irving. The emperor's new drugs: exploding the antidepressant myth. ReadHowYouWant. com, 2010.
40 Whitaker, Robert. Mad in America: Bad science, bad medicine, and the enduring mistreatment of the mentally ill. Basic Books, 2001.
41 Samuels, Robert. "Catharsis: The Politics of Enjoyment." Zizek and the Rhetorical Unconscious. Palgrave Macmillan, Cham, 2020. 7–31.
42 Baldwin, Yael Goldman. Lacan and addiction: An anthology. Routledge, 2018.
43 Lacan, Jacques. "The Subversion of the Subject and the Dialectic of Desire in the Freudian Unconscious." Hegel and Contemporary Continental Philosophy 19.6 (1960): 205–235.
44 Fonagy, Peter. "Thinking about thinking: Some clinical and theoretical considerations in the treatment of a borderline patient." International Journal of Psycho-Analysis 72 (1991): 639–656.
45 Samuels, Robert. "Catharsis: The Politics of Enjoyment." Zizek and the Rhetorical Unconscious. Palgrave Macmillan, Cham, 2020. 7–31.
46 Samuels, Robert. "Logos, Global Justice, and the Reality Principle." Zizek and the Rhetorical Unconscious. Palgrave Macmillan, Cham, 2020. 65–86.

# Chapter 7

# Jordan Peterson and Right-Wing Biological Determinism

As I have argued throughout this book, the question of what makes us human has a profound effect on our understanding of technology, culture, and society. Moreover, our comprehension of ourselves and the world around us is greatly compromised by the repression of psychoanalysis. To further clarify this argument, I will examine Jordan Peterson's *12 Rules for Life*, which offers an interesting mix of animal research, Jungian mysticism, and self-help psychology. Since Peterson is often seen as an intellectual hero of Right-wing white males, it is important to examine why his discourse is so appealing to this influential demographic.[1]

## Humans as Animals

Like so many of the writers and theorists discussed in my book, Peterson tends to erase the difference between humans and other animals. This repression of what makes us human is often tied to his return to traditional social hierarchies, prejudices, and stereotypes. For instance, in the following passage, he equates humans to lobsters in order to show how cultural and psychological dominance is based on biological determinism:

> If a dominant lobster is badly defeated, its brain basically dissolves. Then it grows a new, subordinate's brain—one more appropriate to its new, lowly position. Its original brain just isn't sophisticated to manage the transformation from king to bottom dog without virtually complete dissolution and regrowth. Anyone who has experienced a painful transformation after a serious defeat in romance or career may feel some sense of kinship with the once successful crustacean. (6–7)

Although it may seem absurd to equate a lobster's brain with that of a human, Peterson insists that there is no difference between brains and minds on the one hand and humans and other animals on the other hand.[2] Furthermore, his repression of what makes us human helps him to argue that the way we respond to lost love or a failed career is equivalent to how a

DOI: 10.4324/9781003364610-7

lobster's brain is transformed by losing a fight. In this form of social Darwinism, human traits are projected onto other animals, and this use of the primary processes serves to justify and rationalize social hierarchies.[3]

Peterson's mixture of contemporary science and fantasy-based projections is highlighted when he turns to neurotransmitters to explain male dominance in lobsters and human fictional characters:

> A lobster with high levels of serotonin and low levels of octopamine is a cocky, strutting sort of shellfish, much less likely to back down when challenged. This is because serotonin helps regulate postural flexion. A flexed lobster extends its appendages so that it can look tall and dangerous, like Clint Eastwood in a spaghetti Western. (7)

In comparing a shellfish to an actor in a fictional movie, Peterson seeks to naturalize cultural constructions of masculinity; however, we are forced to ask if he is simply expressing himself in easy-to-understand metaphors, or does he really believe that our current conceptions of gender roles is determined by the same biology shaping other animals?[4]

Since Peterson tends to combine scientific fact with cultural fictions, it is hard to know how seriously he takes his own arguments, but the fact that he continues to return to the same metaphor implies that he represses the difference between humans and other animals just as he ignores the distinction between scientific fact and fiction.[5] Moreover, his work reveals one of the dangers of not understanding what makes us human and different from purely biological entities: Since he equates humans with lobsters, he is able to remove culture, education, and individual psychology from his analysis.[6] Thus, in the following example, he equates the automatic reaction of lobsters to the effects of war trauma and child abuse: "Less provocation is necessary to trigger that reflex in a defeated lobster. You can see an echo of that in the heightened startle reflex characteristic of the soldier or battered child with post-traumatic stress disorder" (7–8). In not differentiating between humans and other animals, psychology and culture is replaced with biology, and one result of this substitution is that psychoanalysis is repressed as drug treatment becomes one of the only ways to deal with chemical imbalances caused by traumatic events.[7]

## New Social Darwinism

Peterson's discourse not only may have a profound effect on how his readers understand human psychology, but his rhetoric implies a very particular type of political ideology: "It's winner-take-all in the lobster world, just as it is in human societies, where the top 1 percent have as much loot as the bottom 50 percent—and where the richest eighty-five people have as much as the bottom three and a half billion" (8). While some critics might condemn this high level of economic inequality, Peterson rationalizes and justifies it by seeing it as the inevitable product of natural processes.[8] Here we see how neuroscience, evolutionary psychology, and behavioral economics all tend to lead to the same political philosophy, which is that our inequalities and hierarchies cannot be changed because they are written into our DNA.[9]

Peterson even goes as far as representing Jesus Christ as a libertarian philosopher driven by biological determinism: "Sometimes it is known as the Matthew Principle (Matthew 25:29), derived from what might be the harshest statement ever attributed to Christ: 'to those who have everything, more will be given; from those who have nothing, everything will be taken.' You truly know you are the Son of God when your dicta apply even to crustaceans" (8–9). The underlying idea here is that Jesus realized that the social hierarchy is determined by our animal nature, and so no matter what we try to do, the powerful will always gain power, while the meek shall never inherit the Earth.[10]

Peterson's naturalization of social dominance is often connected to his discourse concerning the stereotypical roles of men and women, and one possible reason for his great popularity with young males may be his rationalization of patriarchy:

> The female lobsters (who also fight hard for territory during the explicitly maternal stages of their existence) identify the top guy quickly, and become irresistibly attracted to him. This is brilliant strategy, in my estimation. It's also one used by females of many different species, including humans. (9–10)

Peterson's argument is that just as female lobsters are quick to be attracted to the most powerful males, human females are also driven to desire whomever is seen as having a high level of social power.[11] Of course, the underlying message here is that if his male readers want to be considered desirable by females, they need to display their social dominance within the established social hierarchy.[12]

In appealing to traditional gender roles, stereotypes, and prejudices, Peterson not only caters to political conservatives, but he also attracts the approval of reactionary, Right-wing men.[13] Since he combines contemporary science with premodern beliefs, he gives patriarchy an added justification and rationalization.[14] Due to the fact that he does not think we can go against human nature, we have to conform to the social hierarchy, which has been determined by biological forces:

"nature" is "what selects," and the longer a feature has existed the more time it has had to be selected—and to shape life. It does not matter whether that feature is physical and biological, or social and cultural. All that matters, from a Darwinian perspective, is permanence—and the dominance hierarchy, however social or cultural it might appear, has been around for some half a billion years. It's permanent. It's real. (14)

In this use of natural selection, we find the repression of culture, history, politics, and individual subjectivity, which are the very things that make us human.[15] Part of the reason for this rhetoric and political ideology is an underlying desire to escape any sense of responsibility, freedom, guilt, or shame. After all, if we are driven by natural selection to act and think in a certain predetermined way, then there is no reason to think that any alternative to our current social and political world is possible.[16]

Peterson goes as far as claiming, "There is little more natural than culture" (14). In this combination of opposite human categories, the role played by language, history, and subjectivity are once again repressed so that nothing can stand in the way of his theory of pure biological determinism.[17] As he reveals throughout his work, an underlying cause for his whole discourse is his desire to undermine the humanities and social sciences, which he tends to equate with "Cultural Marxism" and fake academic rhetoric.[18] Since these other disciplines do not base their analysis on scientific facts, like natural selection and neurotransmitters, they are seen as being simply hidden modes of political indoctrination.

**Repressing Psychoanalysis**

As I have argued throughout this book, when we fail to grasp what makes us human and simply see ourselves as animals or computers, we tend to lose our ability to change ourselves and the world around us. For Peterson, this form of conservative politics is driven by his desire to equate minds with brains and humans with other animals:

The part of our brain that keeps track of our position in the dominance hierarchy is therefore exceptionally ancient and fundamental. It is a master control system, modulating our perceptions, values, emotions, thoughts and actions. It powerfully affects every aspect of our Being, conscious and unconscious alike. (14)

Like so many neuroscientists and evolutionary psychologists, Peterson replaces the psychoanalytic notion of the unconscious with the simple state of lacking awareness.[19] However, Freud's main claim is that the unconscious is determined by repression, and repression is based on the how we deceive ourselves.[20] Thus, unlike other animals, we have the ability to lie to ourselves and use language in a complex, ambiguous, and ambivalent way. In fact, I have been arguing that Peterson represses his own use of language in order to argue that rhetoric plays no role in a human brain determined by evolution and biology.

Although Freud did insist that we often lie to ourselves in order to protect our own idealized self-image, he also realized that we hide things from ourselves in order to escape tension, shame, and guilt.[21] At times, Peterson does point to this type of self-concealment, but he ties it to the natural acceptance of social hierarchies: "There is an unspeakably primordial calculator, deep within you, at the very foundation of your brain, far below your thoughts and feelings. It monitors exactly where you are positioned in society" (15). From this perspective, humans are no different from other animals, who constantly have to monitor the social hierarchy, yet it should be clear that humans often engage in self-defeating behavior, and they are often unaware of what they really desire and fear.[22] Of course, his type of complexity presented by psychoanalysis cannot be tolerated by a public personality like Peterson who wants to provide easy advice to his adoring fans.[23] For example, in the following passage, he informs his readers, "You are a successful lobster, and the most desirable females line up and vie for your attention" (15). A mode of self-help advice framed by evolutionary psychology and New Age mysticism feeds the discourse of Right-wing and conservative males who want to feel justified for their aggressive attitudes towards females.[24] Furthermore, as we have seen in the incel movement and other online male-dominated discourses, the flip-side of men trying to be powerful in order to attract females is the deep resentment they feel towards females who do not see these men as powerful or attractive.[25]

## Mystical Sexual Politics

A part of the contemporary Right is driven by male resentment of what they see as a feminized culture supporting a nanny state and enforced by a censoring and shaming maternal super-ego.[26] Peterson's discourse feeds this masculine backlash by equating masculinity with order and femininity with chaos:

> Order is where the people around you act according to well-understood social norms, and remain predictable and cooperative. It's the world of social structure, explored territory, and familiarity. The state of Order is typically portrayed, symbolically—imaginatively—as masculine ... Chaos is what emerges more catastrophically when you suddenly find yourself without employment, or are betrayed by a lover. As the antithesis of symbolically masculine order, it's presented imaginatively as feminine. (p. xxv)

This opposition between male order and female chaos is in part derived from Peterson's use of Jungian psychoanalysis.[27] As a theory of the collective unconscious and traditional archetypes, Jung's ideas lend themselves to a discourse that combines science and religion.[28] In contrast to Freud, Jung believes that the unconscious is not the effect of an individual's self-deception; instead, he thinks that we inherit mental images and understandings, which have a universal meaning and structure.[29] This theory of inherited thoughts fits in well with evolutionary psychology and conservative religious beliefs because individual psychology, culture, history, politics, and rhetoric are removed from consideration.

One of the effects of repressing most of things that make us human is that the complexity of human relationships is reduced to a stock body of cliches, stereotypes, and prejudices. In fact, Peterson, himself, reveals why it is so attractive to rely on these simplified generalizations:

> Shared beliefs simplify the world, as well, because people who know what to expect from one another can act together to tame the world. There is perhaps nothing more important than the maintenance of this organization—this simplification. If it's threatened, the great ship of state rocks. (p. xxvii)

Peterson not only valorizes this need to create order by simplifying our understanding of the world but also constantly equates order with masculinity and chaos with the feminine.[30] The underlying idea here is that men gain power and understanding by imposing order on the world through the use of simplified generalizations and prejudices.

Peterson's discourse therefore feeds both conservative and reactionary political ideologies because he rationalizes and naturalizes gender hierarchies as he provides a simplistic worldview centered on traditional beliefs, values, and hierarchies.[31] In fact, he reinforces the Republican notion that we have lost our way, and we need to return to an older world where men dominated women and people knew where they stood in the social hierarchy:[32] "loss of group-centred belief renders life chaotic, miserable, intolerable; presence of group-centred belief makes conflict with other groups inevitable. In the West, we have been withdrawing from our tradition-, religion- and even nation-centred cultures, partly to decrease the danger of group conflict" (p. xxix). Here Peterson echoes the authoritarian call to return to traditional family values, which always entails a return to patriarchy and the sexist debasement of women.[33]

In opposition to this return to an oppressive sexist hierarchy, I have argued that one of the things that makes us human is that our sexual drives are open, which functions to complicate our conceptions of gender. I have also insisted on the need to distinguish our sexuality and social organization of sex from other animals, and when we fail to make these distinctions, we often fall into the same rigid gender binary oppositions that we have seen in Peterson's discourse. It is also vital to stress that this misrepresentation of what makes us human has important political, psychological, and cultural effects. As we have seen, Peterson's drive to equate minds with brains and humans with other animals results in a rationalization of economic and social inequality.[34] Since we are represented as being determined by natural selection to see the world through the lens of an eternal social hierarchy, any efforts to resist or organize for a better world are undermined.

## Psychoanalyzing the Manosphere

It is important to note that Peterson first gained his large public audience by challenging a Canadian rule concerning the use of pronouns for transgender people.[35] By standing up against the governments imposition of what he saw as a form of censorship, he became a darling of what is often called the Alt-Right.[36] While Peterson himself often resists being associated with the Right, we have seen how his theories and rhetoric fit in well with the backlash against minority social movements and what is now called identity politics and political correctness.[37] However, few critics have tried to connect together his use of evolutionary psychology, Jungian philosophy, and Right-wing ideology.

One of the paradoxes of his work is that while much of it does point to a mode of biological determinism that undermines any belief in possible change, another part of his work is focused on giving self-help advice.[38] For instance, he tells his readers, "To stand up straight with your shoulders back is to accept the terrible responsibility of life, with eyes wide open. It means deciding to voluntarily transform the chaos of potential into the realities of habitable order" (27). In calling for the individual to get their act together by taking on a more positive and upright posture, he affirms that people can change from a position of weak submission to one of strong dominance.[39] This combination of biological fatalism and self-help individualism points to the way that contemporary Right-wing ideology often brings together two opposite forces: on the one hand, we are told that we are controlled by our inherited mental programs, and on the other hand, we are encouraged to lift ourselves up from our own bootstraps.[40] This combination of conflicting forces reflects on how the free market is seen as both an organized, bottom-up selection process and the locus of individual freedom.

According to the myth of the invisible hand, by acting in a selfish way, we end up contributing to the common good because if each individual focuses on what they do best, everyone profits at the end.[41] Although, it is easy to show how this theory often fails in reality, it is important to look at how Darwin's theory of evolution is often used to naturalize economic competition and selfish greed.[42] In fact, Marx argued that Darwin derived his theory of natural selection not by looking at nature but by looking at the competitive nature of the British economy.[43] From this perspective, the notion of the survival of the fittest represents an ideology serving to rationalize and naturalize social and economic inequality.

One reason, then, why Right-wing males may be drawn to Peterson's discourse is that it helps them to be insensitive to the suffering caused by capitalistic inequality.[44] Since his theory of evolutionary psychology tells us that there will always be winners and losers, there is no reason to bemoan economic deprivation.[45] Moreover, because it is up to individuals to sink or swim on their own, the cynical acceptance of inequality is coupled with a competition for scarce resources.[46] Of course, what is missing from this entire discourse is the way that humans have built institutions designed to reduce suffering and injustice. Thus, an essential things that makes us different from other animals is that we can apply a system of equality and fairness to the distribution of resources and opportunities.[47]

## Anti-modern

One of the paradoxes of Peterson's work is that he bemoans the way the "postmodernists" base everything on power, but his investment in polarized oppositions only serves to heighten the social imposition of power relations.[48] Thus, when he discusses gender relationships, he almost always draws a stark distinction between who has power and who is disempowered; moreover, the modern liberal idea of suspending power through an emphasis on equality and neutrality is almost entirely absent in his work.[49] In fact, as I have argued throughout this book, one of the things that makes us human and does not show up in the brain scans of isolated individuals is the way we structure social institutions around universal principles, which by definition transcend the individual. By insisting on impersonal rules regulated by an impartial judge, we make a break with nature and evolution.[50]

Not only does Peterson tend to reject the foundations of universal democratic law but he also seeks to repress the importance of modern science by claiming that the modern goal of objectivity robs us of our subjectivity and our shared investment in explanatory stories (33–34). Instead of celebrating the incredible achievements caused by the modern scientific perspective, Peterson seeks to retreat to a combination of pseudo-science and New Age mysticism.[51] Driving this rejection of the modern world is his search for a predetermined order shaped by biology and the collective unconscious.[52] Therefore, in the place of trying to test reality from a neutral perspective, Peterson falls back on preestablished prejudices, stereotypes, and cliches.[53] While his investment in magical thinking and traditional order do reflect one of the things that differentiates us from other animals, his imaginative use of the primary processes blocks him from applying the reality principle and modern scientific reason.[54]

As Freud has shown us, humans have the unique ability to transcend reality by imagining things that do not exist in reality, and yet humans, also have the opposite trait of being able to judge reality from a neutral perspective by suspending our self-interest and pursuit of individual pleasure.[55] In order to do the latter, it is necessary for the human being to abstract itself from the immediate world, and this one of the things other animals are unable to do. While we see this withdrawal from nature and immediacy as an alienating force, it is also a key to what allows us to establish social institutions based on fairness, justice, and universal principles.[56] Since many conservative and Right-wing thinkers, like Peterson, do not value these modern liberal ideals, they are left seeing the world as a purely animalistic competition of individuals shaped by an inevitable social hierarchy.[57]

## Gender Wars

Although Peterson will eventually state that consciousness is supposed to mediate between order and chaos (35), he constantly equates order with masculinity and chaos with femininity in a polarized opposition.[58] In fact, he argues that our masculine order is always being threatened by female chaos, and so there can be no common ground between the sexes (34–35).[59] In this demonization of the feminine, he equates women with the foreign, the strange, monsters, horror, sickness, and basically everything else we may consider to be painful or threatening (35).[60] In contrast, the masculine is associated with established hierarchies, authority, tribes, religion, homes, and countries (35). By developing these extreme oppositions of polarized differences, he creates order by devaluing woman while he also eliminates the possibility of any common ground.[61] He adds that just as our brains are programmed to respond instantly to the sight of snakes, we have an immediate reaction to chaos, which of course is equated with the female (37). This combination of evolutionary psychology and traditional sexism represents one of the most attractive and dangerous aspects of his work since some men are drawn to a theory that justifies their fear of women and their sense of superiority to the other gender.[62]

In drawing from Jung's theories of the collective unconscious and shared archetypes, Peterson argues that we tend to see everything through the lens of the opposition between genders (39).[63] As he indicates, many cultures have sought to divide the world by sexual difference, and so it would be unrealistic to try to suspend this type of thinking (39). However, modern liberal democratic law is based on precisely the ability to bracket the gender opposition by requiring all humans to be protected equally.[64] Even though the fight for gender equality is an on-going fight, the last two hundred years have shown an incredible move away from premodern sexism and patriarchy.[65] However, people like Peterson resist these changes because they are afraid of the chaos might arise if the old order is undermined. It should then not be very surprising if Peterson first made a name for himself by oppositing transgender rights since transgenderism calls into question the very foundations of his philosophy.[66] Due the fact that he sees the world through the lens of a strict gender opposition, any blurring of sexual or gender definitions represents a direct threat to his cherished order.

From a psychoanalytic perspective, we can see how the need to neatly divide the world into a strict gender opposition can result in a regressive paranoid state of delusion where everything has a set meaning.[67] In fact, Freud's first theory of paranoid psychosis was based on the idea that delusions are generated from a threat to gender identity caused by the surfacing of same-sex desires.[68] Although I am not positing that Peterson is himself a psychotic, many people do believe that Jung was dominated by psychotic thinking, and we see this type of delusionary processes in Peterson's claims that women represent chaos and men stand for order: "Chaos—the unknown—is symbolically associated with the feminine. This is partly because all the things we have come to know were born, originally, of the unknown, just as all beings we encounter were born of mothers" (40).[69] Peterson's horror of chaos, the feminine, and the unknown represent a paranoid logic where the entire world is split between opposing forces.[70]

## Freud and Critical Introspection

Once again, it is important to realize that one of the things that makes us human is our ability to imagine things that do not exist, and this ability to think beyond reality helps us to discover new ideas but can also lead us to commit to a false view of ourselves and the world around us.[71] This power of imagination is used by Peterson in his own discourse, but he appears to display very little awareness of his own imagination. In other words, what he lacks is critical introspection and the uniquely human ability to think about our own thinking in a critical and neutral way.[72] Moreover, as Freud showed, the only way for us to truly see if we are deluded or not is if we can take an impartial perspective on our own thinking.[73] This call for neutrality requires the analyst to not judge the patient in therapy with the hope that the patient will stop judging himself or herself.[74]

One reason why I have turned to psychoanalysis to determine what makes us human is that the practice of analysis is centered on this unique ability to develop impartiality towards the self and others.[75] Just as we want our judges to be impartial and our scientists to be unbiased, our modern world is shaped by this special mental attitude, which is not natural or inevitable. However, when we try to base our understanding of human beings on other animals, we lose sight of this special human power. Evolutionary psychology and neuroscience thus run the risk of removing the human from human nature, and one effects of this misunderstanding is that the foundations of modern liberal democracy get called into question.

If we no longer believe that scientists can be objective or judges can be impartial, then we will be tempted to turn to magical thinking or authoritarian leaders to shape our worlds.[76] Furthermore, we have seen how Peterson's discourse feeds a sexist view of the world, which blocks universal human rights and seeks to establish a regressive social order. Through his use of strict binary oppositions and over-generalized claims, Peterson follows the rhetoric of the Right, which is often structured by a borderline splitting between extreme idealization and debasement.[77] One reason for this type of discourse is that it replaces ambiguity, ambivalence, and complexity with rigid categories and judgments.[78] As a mode of polarization, borderline splitting turns the world into a clear distinction between the good "us" and the evil "other." Thus, Peterson equates men with order and females with chaos in order to simplify the social world for himself and his audience.[79]

## Borderline Splitting and Paranoid Projections

According to the psychoanalyst Melanie Klein, infants seek to rid themselves of threatening internal feelings and images by projecting negative representations onto the external world.[80] This very human process of projection is coupled with splitting since the mind has the ability to see the world through strict dichotomies with the use of what Freud called the "primary processes."[81] Since computers and other animals do not think, they do not have mental autonomy, and they cannot split the world into a good self and an evil other. Moreover, in the case of humans, these primitive mental processes also help to shape social systems. Thus, one reason why so many cultures use a strict gender opposition to structure their social hierarchies is that this seemingly clear distinction lends itself to social and psychological meaning, identity, and identification.[82] However, it is important to realize how these gender oppositions rely on primitive mental processes. In fact, we can see culture as a way of controlling and taming the primary processes of the individual.

As Klein articulated, infants are prone to be afraid of the dark and fearful of monsters and other non-existing entities.[83] In reality, what these young children are afraid of is the products of their own imagination. Interestingly, when Peterson defines women as being monsters and representatives of the unknown, he is returning to the primitive imagination of threatening thoughts, feelings, and images. He then uses these primitive representations to shape his view of the social order by combining his own repressed fears and desires with the stereotypes, myths, prejudices, and representations derived from Jungian psychology, Christianity, and ancient mythology. Yet, as a backlash discourse, we can also read his discourse as being shaped by a desire to reverse the postmodern reversal of premodern social hierarchies.[84]

## Backlash Psychology

It is vital to realize that Peterson is not a Christian fundamentalist conservative seeking to return to a social hierarchy based on the Bible.[85] Rather, he is a Right-wing reactionary who desires to protest against postmodern academic discourse, Leftist politics, and social regulation:

> The strong turn towards political correctness in universities has exacerbated the problem ... There are whole disciplines in universities forthrightly hostile towards men. These are the areas of study, dominated by the postmodern/neo-Marxist claim that Western culture, in particular, is an oppressive structure, created by white men to dominate and exclude women (and other select groups). (297)

One of the problematic things about this passage is that Peterson equates Leftist social movements, sophisticated academic theories, and progressive values with the hatred of white men.[86] It is therefore easy to see why so many Right-wing white males would find his discourse so attractive; after all, he is arguing that the real victims of society are the people who have historically had the most power.[87] Furthermore, by equating wildly different groups (postmodernists, Marxists, feminists, gay rights activists) under a single banner of "cultural Marxists," he is able to produce a clearly polarized fight between the good white male heterosexual and the evil other.[88]

Like Donald Trump, Peterson wants to use the threat of political correctness to justify the resentment that white males may feel about a changing society that gives more power to women, minorities, and the LGBQT community.[89] In this drive to defend the self against threatening social forces, we see how humans are not determined by purely instinctual reactions and defenses; instead; human desire is mediated by mental fantasies.[90] Thus, as we have witnessed in Peterson's rhetoric, his understanding of gender and culture is shaped by the way he experiences his aggressive instinct through the lens of primitive processes and cultural representations. Since the object of human drives is always a substitute, our fears and desires are shaped by our mental autonomy and submission to social formations.

On a fundamental basis, Peterson's book seeks to offer a defense to threatened males by rationalizing and naturalizing their privilege and resentment.[91] In turning to animal psychology, he seeks to ground his political ideology in a pseudo-science that is supplemented by a pseudo-psychoanalysis. Of course, this use of other discourses to define nature and evolution represent a very human activity, but his own rhetoric is blind to how it selects and applies only theories that feed his reactionary position. Like most users of pseudo-science, Peterson develops an all-encompassing conspiracy theory to explain the world and his own identity.[92] According to this worldview, men need to take back their rightful place in the natural social hierarchy, and one way that they can do this is by learning self-discipline and understanding how they were made to control others.

## Understanding Sapiens

A possible response to Peterson's discourse is Yuval Harari's *Sapiens*, which also turns to evolutionary psychology, but in this effort to define what truly makes us human, the result is not a naturalization of inequality and sexism; rather, Harari seeks to show how our unique ability to create and share believable fictions has resulted in cooperation and the building of long-lasting dynamic societies.[93] For Harari, the fundamental thing that separates us from other animals is our use of language and imagination:

> It's the ability to transmit information about things that do not exist at all. As far as we know, only Sapiens can talk about entire kinds of entities that they have never seen, touched or smelled. Legends, myths, gods and religions appeared for the first time with the Cognitive Revolution. (24)

In this description of what has separated us from other animals, Harari stresses the combination of that Freud called the primary processes and transference. Not only are we able to imagine things that do not exist, but we are also able to believe the imagined representations of others.[94]

By transcending reality and communicating fictional representations, humans are able to cooperate on a mass scale, which ultimately leads to the pooling of resources and the extension of human life: "Sapiens can cooperate in extremely flexible ways with countless numbers of strangers. That's why Sapiens rule the world, whereas ants eat our leftovers and chimps are locked up in zoos and research laboratories" (25). According to this theory, our combined use of language and imagination has helped us to work together and transcend the state of other animals and beings. Moreover, while Peterson stresses the way that evolution places males in a position of dominance, Harari seeks to separate us from other animals by revealing how our mental autonomy, communication skills, and free will lead us to higher levels of social organization and group equality:

> Our chimpanzee cousins usually live in small troops of several dozen individuals. They form close friendships, hunt together and fight shoulder to shoulder against baboons, cheetahs and enemy chimpanzees. Their social structure tends to be hierarchical. The dominant member, who is almost always a male, is termed the 'alpha male.' Other males and females exhibit their submission to the alpha male by bowing before him while making grunting sounds, not unlike human subjects kowtowing before a king. (25)

Although there is often a human tendency to create social hierarchies based on gender differences, a key driving force of historical progress is our ability to break with this type of animalistic natural order.[95]

While Peterson focuses on opposition and hierarchy, Harari tends to look for the ways people are able to work together by sharing fictional representations:

> Any large-scale human cooperation—whether a modern state, a medieval church, an ancient city or an archaic tribe—is rooted in common myths that exist only in people's collective imagination ... Two lawyers who have never met can nevertheless combine efforts to defend a complete stranger because they both believe in the existence of laws, justice, human rights—and the money paid out in fees. (27–28)

Although the sharing of common myths can lead to both highly destructive and highly productive results, the possibility of human rights and democratic justice relies on the ability of sharing beliefs based on fictional representations. In fact, I have argued that the ideals of universality and impartiality are necessary but impossible because they can never be fully attained; however, these beliefs and fictions serve to structure our fundamental human institutions. As Harari implies, the key to social progress is cooperation, which acts to go beyond the brains and nature of isolated individuals, and it this form of collective power, which is often rejected by Right-wing thinkers like Peterson.[96]

Since other animals cannot think or imagine things that do not exist, they are unable to work together on the same scale as human beings: "Yet none of these things exists outside the stories that people invent and tell one another. There are no gods in the universe, no nations, no money, no human rights, no laws, and no justice outside the common imagination of human beings" (28). This power to create and believe in fictional representations is our greatest strength and weakness as human beings, and it is in part due to this power of imagination that Freud sought to counter the primary processes with reality testing and impartial science.[97] However, when we fail to distinguish what makes us human, we are no longer able to understand their power of our minds and the need to limit this power for the collective good.

## Notes

1 van de Ven, Inge, and Ties van Gemert. "Filter bubbles and guru effects: Jordan B. Peterson as a public intellectual in the attention economy." *Celebrity Studies* 13.3 (2022): 289–307.
2 Clark, Gary. "Carl Jung, John Layard and Jordan Peterson: Assessing Theories of Human Social Evolution and Their Implications for Analytical Psychology." *International Journal of Jungian Studies* 12.2 (2020): 129–158.
3 Burgis, Ben, et al. *Myth and Mayhem: A Leftist Critique of Jordan Peterson*. John Hunt Publishing, 2020.
4 Stove, Judy. "Why Jordan Peterson matters: Virtue and naturalistic morality." *Quadrant* 62.10 (2018): 54–58.

5 Manne, Kate. "Reconsider the lobster: Jordan Peterson's failed antidote for'toxic masculine despair'." *TLS. Times Literary Supplement* 6008 (2018): 14–16.
6 Burston, Daniel. "It's hip to be square! The myths of Jordan Peterson." *Psychotherapy and Politics International* 17.1 (2019): e1475.
7 van de Ven, Inge, and Ties van Gemert. "Filter bubbles and guru effects: Jordan B. Peterson as a public intellectual in the attention economy." *Celebrity Studies* 13.3 (2022): 289–307.
8 Samuels, Robert. *Psychoanalyzing the politics of the new brain sciences.* Springer, 2017.
9 Richerson, Peter J., and Robert Boyd. *Not by genes alone: How culture transformed human evolution.* University of Chicago press, 2008.
10 Keneally, Kristina. "The prosperity Gospel: Correspondence." *Quarterly Essay* 75 (2019): 95–99.
11 Nesbitt-Larking, Paul. "Constructing narratives of masculinity: Online followers of Jordan B. Peterson." *Psychology of Men & Masculinities* (2022).
12 Demetriou, Dan. "Virgin Versus Chad: On Enforced Monogamy as a Solution to the Incel Problem." *The Palgrave Handbook of Sexual Ethics.* Palgrave Macmillan, Cham, 2022. 155–175.
13 Manne, Kate. "Reconsider the lobster: Jordan Peterson's failed antidote for'toxic masculine despair'." *TLS. Times Literary Supplement* 6008 (2018): 14–16.
14 Beckner, Stephen. "Thought crimes: Jordan Peterson and the meaning of the meaning of life." *Skeptic (Altadena, CA)* 23.3 (2018): 26–35.
15 Feldmann, John Ryan. "Order Out of Chaos: The Political Theology of Jordan Peterson." *Stasis* 10.2 (2020).
16 Rowson, Jonathan. "An Epistemic Thunderstorm: What We Learned and Failed to Learn from Jordan Peterson's Rise to Fame." *An Epistemic Thunderstorm: What We Learned and Failed to Learn* 16.2 (2020).
17 Clark, Gary. "Carl Jung, John Layard and Jordan Peterson: Assessing Theories of Human Social Evolution and Their Implications for Analytical Psychology." *International Journal of Jungian Studies* 12.2 (2020): 129–158.
18 Mirrlees, Tanner. "The Alt-right's Discourse on" Cultural Marxism": A Political Instrument of Intersectional Hate." *Atlantis: critical studies in gender, culture & social justice* 39.1 (2018): 49–69.
19 Burston, Daniel. *Psychoanalysis, politics and the Postmodern University.* London: Palgrave Macmillan, 2020.
20 Freud, Sigmund. "Repression." *The Standard Edition of the Complete Psychological Works of Sigmund Freud, Volume XIV (1914–1916): On the History of the Psycho-Analytic Movement, Papers on Metapsychology and Other Works.* 1957. 141–158.
21 Freud, Sigmund. "Project for a scientific psychology (1950 [1895])." *The Standard Edition of the Complete Psychological Works of Sigmund Freud, Volume I (1886–1899): Pre-Psycho-Analytic Publications and Unpublished Drafts.* 1966. 281–391.
22 Samuels, Robert. "Freud's Project." *(Mis) Understanding Freud with Lacan, Zizek, and Neuroscience.* Palgrave Macmillan, Cham, 2022. 7–28.
23 Stea, Jonathan N. "Jordan Peterson's Endeavor." *Skeptic (Altadena, CA)* 23.3 (2018): 25–26.
24 Dafaure, Maxime. "Memes, trolls and the manosphere: mapping the manifold expressions of antifeminism and misogyny online." *European Journal of English Studies* 26.2 (2022): 236–254.

25 Maloney, Marcus, Steve Roberts, and Callum Jones. "'How do I become blue pilled?': Masculine ontological insecurity on 4chan's advice board." *new media & society* (2022): 14614448221103124.
26 Sugiura, Lisa. *The incel rebellion: The rise of the manosphere and the virtual war against women.* Emerald Group Publishing, 2021.
27 Lahiki, Malena Granhall, and Sarah Ljungquist. "Masculinity in the Populist Manichean Mindset." *Populism, Democracy, and the Humanities: Interdisciplinary Explorations and Critical Enquiries* (2022): 93.
28 Peterson, Jordan B. *Maps of meaning: The architecture of belief.* Routledge, 2002.
29 Jung, Carl Gustav. *The archetypes and the collective unconscious.* Routledge, 2014.
30 McLaughlin, Neil. "The Jordan Peterson Phenomena: Why Fromm's ideas and public intellectual vision is essential for responding to reactionary populism." *Fromm Forum (English Edition–ISSN 1437–1189), 25/2021, Tuebingen (Selbstverlag), pp. 074–089.* Vol. 25. 2021.
31 Feldmann, John Ryan. "Order Out of Chaos: The Political Theology of Jordan Peterson." *Stasis* 10.2 (2020).
32 Brooks, Michael. *Against the web: A cosmopolitan answer to the new right.* John Hunt Publishing, 2020.
33 Grewal, Inderpal. "Authoritarian Patriarchy and Its Populism." *English Studies in Africa* 63.1 (2020): 179–198.
34 Whitham, Ben. "A postmodern neo-Marxist's guide to free speech: Jordan Peterson, the alt-right and neo-fascism." *The free speech wars.* Manchester University Press, 2020. 227–238.
35 Holmes, Andy, and Phebe Ferrer. "Canadian Bill C-16: Decolonizing the Protection of Two-Spirit, Gender Non-Binary and Transgender People." *2018.*: 13.
36 Southey, Tabatha. "Is Jordan Peterson the stupid man's smart person?." *Macleans, November* 17 (2017): 2017.
37 Samuels, Robert. "The Backlash Politics of Evolutionary Psychology: Steven Pinker's Blank Slate." *Psychoanalyzing the politics of the new brain sciences.* Palgrave Pivot, Cham, 2017. 35–58.
38 Stea, Jonathan N. "Jordan Peterson's Endeavor." *Skeptic (Altadena, CA)* 23.3 (2018): 25–26.
39 McLaughlin, Neil. "Jordan Peterson, Beyond Order: 12 More Rules for Life." (2021): 447–452.
40 Silvers, Stuart. "Methodological and moral muddles in evolutionary psychology." *The Journal of Mind and Behavior* (2010): 65–83.
41 Rothschild, Emma. "Adam Smith and the invisible hand." *The American Economic Review* 84.2 (1994): 319–322.
42 Amir-ud-Din, Rafi, and Asad Zaman. "Failures of the "Invisible Hand"." *Forum for Social Economics.* Vol. 45. No. 1. Routledge, 2016.
43 Gerratana, Valentino. "Marx and Darwin." *New Left Review* 82 (1973): 60–82.
44 Crociani-Windland, Lita, and Candida Yates. "Masculinity, affect and the search for certainty in an age of precarity." *Free Associations* 78 (2020): 119–140.
45 Daly, Martin. "Evolutionary psychology and inequality." *Evolutionary Behavioral Sciences* 14.4 (2020): 324.
46 Petersen, Michael Bang, et al. "Who deserves help? Evolutionary psychology, social emotions, and public opinion about welfare." *Political psychology* 33.3 (2012): 395–418.

47 Samuels, Robert. "The Brain Sciences Against the Welfare State." *Psychoanalyzing the Politics of the New Brain Sciences.* Palgrave Pivot, Cham, 2017. 85–114.
48 Raatikainen, Panu. "Jordan Peterson on Postmodernism, Truth, and Science." (2022).
49 Samuels, Robert. "Logos, global justice, and the reality principle." *Zizek and the rhetorical unconscious.* Palgrave Macmillan, Cham, 2020. 65–86.
50 Samuels, Robert. *The Psychopathology of Political Ideologies.* Routledge, 2021.
51 Dennen, David. "Politics and prophecy: Jordan Peterson's antidote to modernity." (2019).
52 Nicholls, Brett. "Postmodernism in the Twenty-First Century: Jordan Peterson, Jean Baudrillard and the Problem of Chaos." *Post-Truth and the Mediation of Reality.* Palgrave Macmillan, Cham, 2019. 57–77.
53 Champagne, Marc. *Myth, Meaning, and Antifragile Individualism: On the Ideas of Jordan Peterson.* Vol. 69. Andrews UK Limited, 2020.
54 Samuels, Robert. "Science and the reality principle." *Freud for the twenty-first century.* Palgrave Pivot, Cham, 2019. 5–16.
55 Freud, Sigmund. "Formulations on the two principles of mental functioning." *The Standard Edition of the Complete Psychological Works of Sigmund Freud, Volume XII (1911–1913): The Case of Schreber, Papers on Technique and Other Works.* 1958. 213–226.
56 Samuels, Robert. "Logos, global justice, and the reality principle." *Zizek and the rhetorical unconscious.* Palgrave Macmillan, Cham, 2020. 65–86.
57 Chappell, John E. "Social Darwinism, environmentalism, and ideology." *Annals of the Association of American Geographers* 83.1 (1993): 160–163.
58 Shermer, Michael. "Have Archetype--Will Travel: The Jordan Peterson Phenomenon." *Skeptic (Altadena, CA)* 23.3 (2018): 19–25.
59 Veissière, Samuel Paul Louis. ""Toxic Masculinity" in the age of# MeToo: ritual, morality and gender archetypes across cultures." *Society and Business Review* (2018).
60 Kelsey, Darren. "Archetypal Populism: The "Intellectual Dark Web" and the "Peterson Paradox"." *Discursive Approaches to Populism Across Disciplines.* Palgrave Macmillan, Cham, 2020. 171–198.
61 Feldmann, John Ryan. "Order Out of Chaos: The Political Theology of Jordan Peterson." *Stasis* 10.2 (2020).
62 Dafaure, Maxime. "Memes, trolls and the manosphere: mapping the manifold expressions of antifeminism and misogyny online." *European Journal of English Studies* 26.2 (2022): 236–254.
63 McLaughlin, Neil. "The Jordan Peterson Phenomena: Why Fromm's ideas and public intellectual vision is essential for responding to reactionary populism." *Fromm Forum (English Edition–ISSN 1437–1189), 25/2021, Tuebingen (Selbstverlag), pp. 074–089.* Vol. 25. 2021.
64 Deveaux, Monique. *Gender and justice in multicultural liberal states.* Oup Oxford, 2006.
65 Case, Mary Anne. "Reflections on constitutionalizing women's equality." *California Law Review* 90.3 (2002): 765–790.
66 Guignion, David. "Jordan Peterson and the (F) law of 'Scientific Inquiry': A Critical Evaluation of Peterson's Use of Science and Philosophy in His Conquest Against Social Justice." *Politikon: The IAPSS Journal of Political Science* 41 (2019): 7–23.
67 Freud, Sigmund. "Some neurotic mechanisms in jealousy, paranoia, and homosexuality." *Gender & Envy.* Routledge, 2014. 213–220.

68 Freud, Sigmund. *Psycho-analytic notes on an autobiographical account of a case of paranoia (dementia paranoides)*. Read Books Ltd, 2014.
69 Eigen, Michael. *The psychotic core*. Routledge, 2018.
70 Vila-Badia, Regina, et al. "Cognitive functioning in first episode psychosis. Gender differences and relation with clinical variables." *Early intervention in psychiatry* 15.6 (2021): 1667–1676.
71 Samuels, Robert. "The unconscious and the primary processes." *Freud for the twenty-first century*. Palgrave Pivot, Cham, 2019. 27–42.
72 Wolf, Ernest, S., and John, E. Gedo. "The last introspective psychologist before Freud: Michel de Montaigne." *Annual of Psychoanalysis* 3 (1975): 297–310.
73 Samuels, Robert. "Science and the reality principle." *Freud for the twenty-first century*. Palgrave Pivot, Cham, 2019. 5–16.
74 Poland, Warren S. "On the analyst's neutrality." *Journal of the American Psychoanalytic Association* 32.2 (1984): 283–299.
75 de la Torre, Jorge. "Psychoanalytic neutrality: an overview." *Bulletin of the Menninger Clinic* 41.4 (1977): 366.
76 Rensmann, Lars. *The politics of unreason: The Frankfurt School and the origins of modern antisemitism*. Suny Press, 2017.
77 Fertuck, Eric A., Stephanie Fischer, and Joseph Beeney. "Social cognition and borderline personality disorder: splitting and trust impairment findings." *Psychiatric Clinics* 41.4 (2018): 613–632.
78 Gallop, Ruth. "The patient is splitting: Everyone knows and nothing changes." *Journal of Psychosocial Nursing and Mental Health Services* 23.4 (1985): 6–9.
79 Samuels, Robert. "Catharsis: The politics of enjoyment." *Zizek and the rhetorical unconscious*. Palgrave Macmillan, Cham, 2020. 7–31.
80 Klein, Melanie. "Notes on some schizoid mechanisms3." *Projective Identification*. Routledge, 2013. 19–46.
81 Klein, Melanie. "Our adult world and its roots in infancy." *Human Relations* 12.4 (1959): 291–303.
82 Derks, Belle, and Naomi Ellemers. "Gender and social hierarchies: introduction and overview." *Gender and Social Hierarchies*. Routledge, 2015. 13–20.
83 Klein, Melanie. "On the development of mental functioning." *International Journal of Psycho-Analysis* 39 (1958): 84–90.
84 McLaughlin, Neil. "The two Jacobys: Contradiction, ironies and challenges in new left critical social psychology after Jordan Peterson." *Free Associations: Psychoanalysis and Culture, Media, Groups, Politics, No. 72 (June 2018)*. http://www.freeassociations.org.uk/ (2018).
85 Huntington, Samuel P. "Conservatism as an Ideology." *American political science review* 51.2 (1957): 454–473.
86 Klein, Daniel B. "On Jordan Peterson, Postmodernism, and PoMo-Bashing." *Society* 55.6 (2018): 477–481.
87 Manne, Kate. "Reconsider the lobster: Jordan Peterson's failed antidote for'toxic masculine despair'." *TLS. Times Literary Supplement* 6008 (2018): 14–16.
88 Mirrlees, Tanner. "The Alt-right's Discourse on" Cultural Marxism": A Political Instrument of Intersectional Hate." *Atlantis: critical studies in gender, culture & social justice* 39.1 (2018): 49–69.
89 Samuels, Robert. "Victim politics: Psychoanalyzing the neoliberal conservative counter-revolution." *Psychoanalyzing the left and right after Donald Trump*. Palgrave Macmillan, Cham, 2016. 7–29.
90 Žižek, Slavoj. "The seven veils of fantasy." *Key concepts of Lacanian psycho-analysis*. Routledge, 2018. 190–218.

91  Dyson, Michael Eric, et al. *Political Correctness: The Munk Debates*. House of Anansi, 2018.
92  Burgis, Ben, et al. *Myth and Mayhem: A Leftist Critique of Jordan Peterson*. John Hunt Publishing, 2020.
93  Harari, Yuval Noah. *Sapiens: A Brief History of Humankind*. Random House, 2014.
94  Dowdy, Art. "Survival Contingencies: A Review of Sapiens: A Brief History of Humankind by Yuval Noah Harari." *Perspectives on Behavior Science* 43.1 (2020): 233–242.
95  Olstein, Diego Adrián, and Yuval N. Harari. *Thinking history globally*. Londres: Palgrave Macmillan, 2015.
96  Araki, Naoki. "Sapiens and Language." *Bulletin of Hiroshima Institute of Technology* 53 (2019): 1–10.
97  Samuels, Robert. "Logos, global justice, and the reality principle." *Zizek and the rhetorical unconscious*. Palgrave Macmillan, Cham, 2020. 65–86.

# Chapter 8

# Conclusion: Why Defining the Human Matters

This book has argued that psychoanalysis helps us to understand what makes us human. Through our break with nature, reality, and evolution, humans are able to transcend both their internal and external nature. These separations not only differentiate us from other animals and machines, but they also point to how we may be able to resolve some of the most pressing individual and social problems. As I pointed out in previous chapters, one of the biggest challenges for humans is that we are driven to pursue pleasure, and this drive for enjoyment represents an escape from tension, anxiety, guilt, shame, and ultimately reality itself. The fact that we can turn any process or object into a mode of enjoyment means that we are prone to addictive behavior and self-defeating thoughts and actions. In fact, I have posited that the greatest threat to humanity may be our propensity to deny reality, and due to this denial, we may be unable to directly confront global problems like climate change, pandemics, war, and dire poverty.[1]

In the case of the political responses to the COVID-19 pandemic, we have seen that some people would rather risk their lives and the lives of others in order to hold onto the fantasy of total freedom and enjoyment.[2] Due to the growing dominance of a libertarian Right-wing ideology, people seek to protect their pursuit of pleasure, even if it leads to death.[3] Just as Freud showed how the pleasure principle ends up producing a death drive, the human desire to be free from all social control and regulation can lead to self-destruction and the death of our shared environment.[4]

The pleasure principle also helps us to see why some people may not respond to the most pressing personal and social issues because they have become addicted to easy pleasure derived from media technologies. As a form of auto-erotism, this direct access to enjoyment bypasses the need for social relationships and the acceptance of a shared reality.[5] Just as the neoliberal ideologues claim that there is no such thing as society, and all we have is the competition between separate individuals, the person addicted to opiates or immersed in binge watching feels that the tension caused by the conflict between society and the individual can be eliminated or avoided.[6]

DOI: 10.4324/9781003364610-8

Although pandemics like COVID-19 should force us to see that we are all connected, and everything we do can affect other people, many choose to reject this need for social understanding, and instead, they desire to see their lives in terms of individual rights and preferences.[7] Politicians on the Right have fed into this selfish way of thinking by positing that the only things that matter is free speech, the free market, and the free individual. As a form of the death drive, people are willing to risk their lives and the lives of others in order to pursue their narrow self-interest.[8] In fact, we have also seen how the new brain sciences tend to reinforce this ideology by arguing that we are controlled by our selfish genes, whose only goal is to self-replicate and compete with other genes for scarce reproductive opportunities.[9] This new mode of social Darwinism results in biological determinism in the form of what I have called neo-animism.[10]

Following Freud's notion that the original state of civilization was animistic because internal mental states were experienced as external reality, I have shown how many brain scientists and evolutionary psychologists treat animals and computers like people and people like computers and non-human animals.[11] This projection of human thought onto external reality is connected to our desire to outsource all of our mental functions so that computers can do our thinking for us. Not only are we driven to automate all of our labor, but we also seek to externalize our minds by downloading our mental functions into the Web and the cloud.[12] It is as if we have a desperate desire to escape from our own minds. In fact, Freud argued that the pleasure principle entails a law of mental inertia, which drives us to use as little mental energy as possible.[13] The ultimate end point of this drive is death itself as we seek to return to a state of inanimation.[14] Therefore, at the very moment we are projecting life onto machines, we are trying to eliminate our own lives by ridding ourselves of any excitement or tension.

The reason then why some governments forced their people to get back to work and risk their lives during a pandemic is that the dominance of the pleasure principle in our culture entails the drive to act without a concern for life. People are not only being asked to choose between their jobs and their lives, but the entire healthcare system in the United States is so fixated on the profit-motive that instead of making the saving of lives the top priority, hospitals have to fight over scarce resources to respond to an ongoing crisis.[15]

What in part drives people and governments to not respond to a global crisis like the COVID-19 pandemic is the way our minds allow us to replace reality with imagined representations. Since humans are able to transcend reality through their conscious thoughts, they are prone to engage in magical thinking, like conspiracy theories, or the hope that the virus will just disappear on its own.[16] Psychoanalysis tells us that not only is our consciousness shaped by ideas divorced from material reality, but language allows us to lie to ourselves and repress our own consciousness into our unconscious.[17]

At a time when we need to make decisions based on science and facts, we are constantly witnessing public officials suspend reason as they rely on ideology to interpret the world. This reaction to the modern Enlightenment is one of the greatest threats to global progress, and it is in part based on the notion that science can never be objective and neutral, and so it must always be biased and based on cultural differences and personal self-interest.[18] Instead of following Freud's notions of neutrality, universality, and the reality principle as the foundation of science, many people on the Left and the Right tend to discard the necessary but impossible ideals of objectivity and impartiality.[19] It therefore becomes very difficult to respond to a health crisis, if people no longer trust or understand science.[20]

Part of this movement away from reason and science is due to the way our media tend to combine information with entertainment and business.[21] In other words, since journalists now often have to attract an audience to make money, they are motivated to tell people the things that either excite them or scare them.[22] Making matters worse, many news outlets cater to a particular political ideology, and so there really is little fair and balanced reporting.[23] One of the results of these media trends is that people do not know whom to trust, and they are prone to conspiracy theories and ideological mis-representations. It is therefore important to understand that not only humans are able to escape reality but we also have to comprehend what allows us to best approximate what is really going on in the world.

As I have argued throughout this book, psychoanalysis is grounded on the idea that we cannot completely escape our inner or outer conflicts, and so we must free ourselves to acknowledge the truth of our existence.[24] This radical self-honesty has to be coupled with the acknowledgment that there are limits to our knowledge, and ultimately we will never have a full grasp of the real. In fact, Freud posited that what differentiates science from religion and animism is that with science, we accept the limitations of our knowledge as we affirm the necessity of nature.[25] Freud added that in the case of animism, people project their own inner thoughts onto the outer world, and one reason they do this is that they have little understanding about how their minds actually work. What is so interesting and upsetting about the new brain sciences is that they often represent a return to animism in the way they project thoughts onto external objects and beings. Not only do these pseudo-scientists use non-human animals to understand the human mind, but also they represent their knowledge from a totalizing perspective.[26] This lack of cognitive humility goes against Freud's claim that modern science only really starts when we make a break with the "omnipotence of thoughts."[27]

We have seen that in the effort to ground our understanding of the mind in evolutionary biology, the new brain scientists have to repress the very things that make us human. By trying to escape history, politics, social mediation, culture, and subjectivity, scientism provides a sense of certainty while it obscures our humanity.[28] Since neuroscience and evolutionary psychology tend to represent humans as computers programmed by natural selection, the only solution to our personal and social problems becomes drug treatment, and this turn toward pharmacology represents the dominance of the pleasure principle's death drive.[29] It turns out that one of the results of our technological and cultural development is that we are better able to satisfy our urge for self-destruction.

Although some people believe that our encounters with a global pandemic will help us to realize that we need to work together to fight global climate change, psychoanalysis helps us to see that people may not care about the environment or their own health because they are driven to destroy themselves in their pursuit of pleasure and freedom.[30] The paradox of this libertarian focus on liberty is that it ends up making us slaves to social and psychological forces that we refuse to address. For instance, we have seen that when scientists turn to biological determinism, they often not only erase free will but also blind us from seeing all of the different social and cultural forces shaping our lives.[31]

It is important to realize that the reason why the new brain sciences have a hard time defining free will and consciousness is that they have repressed psychoanalysis and the human break from reality and instincts. This is not just an academic dispute because it has consequences in the real world. After all, if we really believe that free will does not exist, and we are determined by evolution, why should be motivated to address any personal or social problems? If our genes make us do everything, then there is really no need for political interventions or a conscious understanding of the world around us.[32] However, I have tried to show that not only do we have free will and consciousness, but we have created social institutions built on the necessary but impossible ideals of reason, universality, and impartiality.[33] These social formations may not show up in the brain scans of isolated individuals or in the reactions of tested nonhuman animals, and yet, they help to define what makes us human and how we can promote justice and prosperity.

Since no one can act as if the law does not matter, social norms and regulations transcend our individual consciousness. Moreover, reason and reality testing require critical introspection so that we suspend our biases and self-interests. For Freud, psychoanalysis is a true science because it not only pushes us to apply impartial reason to our understanding of the world around us, but it also provides a way of taking a neutral perspective on our own thoughts, feelings, and memories.[34] Through the neutrality of the analyst and the free association of the patent, a way is found to suspend the pleasure principle and to confront the conflicts shaping ourselves and our world. Psychoanalysis also works against our tendency to transfer responsibility onto others. By working through the transference in analysis, we come to realize that our fundamental demand to others is based on our attempt to make others responsible for knowledge, love, and recognition.[35] Freud added that religion is ultimately a middle ground between animism and science because in religious prayer, we create an imaginary Other who we hope to influence through our demands.[36]

In refusing to respond to the demands of the patient, the analyst opens up a space for people to see how what they really want is for others to submit to their will. Therefore, when the baby cries in order to get milk, the baby is not just seeking to receive recognition, knowledge, and love from the Other; what the subject really desires is for the Other to submit to the subject's desire.[37] One reason for this structure is that our freedom and pleasure is often predicated on others giving up their freedom and enjoyment.[38] Our desire to submit to a higher power is then also a desire for that power to submit to us by answering our prayers or demands. Psychoanalysis offers a way to get past this dynamic by creating an artificial situation where the one who receives our demands refuses to respond and satisfy them. Through a process of optimal frustration, people learn to break their dependency on imaginary saviors. Unfortunately, many therapists and psychoanalysis do not understand how analysis works, and so they end up re-enforcing the transference instead of helping to eliminate it.

In terms of politics and our ability to counter threats like climate change and global pandemics, we need to trust and apply science as we stop believing in people who pretend to have all of the answers. Part of this process relies on understanding how science functions and what reason really means.[39] As I have shown throughout this work, this understanding of science and reason is blocked in part by the development of the new brain sciences that repress what makes us human and misunderstand the true essence of science itself. As a fundamental way of breaking with the pleasure principle, magical thinking, and transference, science has to be understood as the impartial application of a shared symbolic logic to a reality that can never be fully known.[40] The reason, then, why science is based on a set of necessary but impossible ideals is that the concepts of neutrality, universality, and objectivity are human constructions that drive our social behavior and are never completely achieved.[41] These ideals do not exist in nature, and they are not products of evolution; instead, universal human rights and scientific reason have been developed through constant social negotiation, testing, and revision. As works in progress, science and democracy promote a dynamic universality that feeds our global progress and helps to determine what makes us human.

## Notes

1  Samuels, Robert. "Catharsis: The Politics of Enjoyment." *Zizek and the Rhetorical Unconscious*. Palgrave Macmillan, Cham, 2020. 7–31.
2  Falkenbach, Michelle, and Scott L. Greer. "Denial and Distraction: How the Populist Radical Right Responds to COVID-19; Comment on "a Scoping review of PRR parties' Influence on Welfare Policy and its Implication for Population Health in Europe"." *International journal of health policy and management* (2020).

3 Block, Walter. "A Libertarian Analysis of the COVID-19 Pandemic." *Journal of Libertarian Studies* 24.1 (2020): 206–237.

4 Boothby, Richard. *Death and Desire (RLE: Lacan): Psychoanalytic Theory in Lacan's Return to Freud*. Routledge, 2014.

5 Freud, Sigmund. *Civilization and its Discontents*. Broadview Press, 2015.

6 Samuels, Robert. "The Pleasure Principle and the Death Drive." *Freud for the Twenty-First Century*. Palgrave Pivot, Cham, 2019. 17–25.

7 Ruiz, Rosaura Martínez. "Introduction: After Beyond … ? Freud's Death Drive and the Future of a Better World." (2020): 1–4.

8 Iyer, Ravi, et al. "Understanding Libertarian Morality: The Psychological Roots of an Individualist Ideology." *Available at SSRN 1665934* (2010).

9 Midgley, Mary. *The Solitary Self: Darwin and the Selfish Gene*. Routledge, 2014.

10 Bouissac, Paul. "What Is a Human? Ecological Semiotics and the New Animism." *Semiotica* 77.4 (1989): 497–516.

11 Billig, Michael. "Commodity Fetishism and Repression: Reflections on Marx, Freud and the Psychology of Consumer Capitalism." *Theory & Psychology* 9.3 (1999): 313–329.

12 Arnol'd, Vladimir Igorevich, Vladimir Igorevič Arnol'd, and V. I. Arnold. *Singularity Theory*. Vol. 53. Cambridge University Press, 1981.

13 Freud, Sigmund. "Project for a Scientific Psychology (1950 [1895])." *The Standard Edition of the Complete Psychological Works of Sigmund Freud, Volume I (1886–1899): Pre-Psycho-Analytic Publications and Unpublished Drafts*. 1966. 281–391.

14 Freud, Sigmund. *Beyond the Pleasure Principle*. Penguin UK, 2003.

15 Metzl, Jonathan M., Aletha Maybank, and Fernando De Maio. "Responding to the COVID-19 Pandemic: The Need for a Structurally Competent Health Care System." *JAMA* (2020).

16 Atkinson, Christopher L., et al. "Supply Chain Manipulation, Misrepresentation, and Magical Thinking During the COVID-19 Pandemic." *The American Review of Public Administration* 50.6-7 (2020): 628–634.

17 Schafer, Roy. "Self-deception, Defense, and Narration." *Psychoanalysis and Contemporary Thought* 10.3 (1987): 319–346.

18 Marín, Francesc-Xavier, Jordi Rusiñol, and Josep Gallifa. "Pseudoscientific Beliefs and Psychopathological Risks Increase after COVID-19 Social Quarantine." *Globalization and Health* 16.1 (2020): 1–11.

19 Samuels, Robert. "Science and the Reality Principle." *Freud for the Twenty-First Century*. Palgrave Pivot, Cham, 2019. 5–16.

20 Martin, Graham P., et al. "Science, Society, and Policy in the Face of Uncertainty: Reflections on the Debate around Face Coverings for the Public During COVID-19." *Critical Public Health* (2020): 1–8.

21 Thussu, Daya Kishan. *News as Entertainment: The Rise of Global Infotainment*. Sage, 2007.

22 Lee, GangHeong, Joseph N. Cappella, and Brian Southwell. "The Effects of News and Entertainment on Interpersonal Trust: Political TalkRadio, Newspapers, and Television." *Mass Communication and Society* 6.4 (2003): 413–434.

23 Spohr, Dominic. "Fake News and Ideological Polarization: Filter Bubbles and Selective Exposure on Social Media." *Business Information Review* 34.3 (2017): 150–160.

24 Wallwork, Ernest. *Psychoanalysis and Ethics*. Yale University Press, 1991.

25 Freud, Sigmund. *Totem and Taboo: Resemblances between the Psychic Lives of Savages and Neurotics*. Good Press, 2019.

26  Hacker, P. M. S. "Philosophy and Scientism: What Cognitive Neuroscience Can, and What It Cannot, Explain." *Scientism: The new orthodoxy* (2015): 97–115.
27  Freud, Sigmund. *The Future of an Illusion*. Broadview Press, 2012.
28  Williams, Richard N., and Daniel N. Robinson, eds. *Scientism: The New Orthodoxy*. Bloomsbury Publishing, 2014.
29  Samuels, Robert. "Drugging Discontent: Psychoanalysis, Drives, and the Governmental University Medical Pharmaceutical Complex (GUMP)." *Psychoanalyzing the Politics of the New Brain Sciences*. Palgrave Pivot, Cham, 2017. 115–136.
30  Manzanedo, Rubén D., and Peter Manning. "COVID-19: Lessons for the Climate Change Emergency." *Science of the Total Environment* 742 (2020): 140563.
31  Lewontin, Richard C., Steven Rose, and Leon J. Kamin. *Not in Our Genes*. New York: Pantheon Books, 1984.
32  Stanovich, Keith E., and Richard F. West. "Evolutionary versus Instrumental Goals: How Evolutionary Psychology Misconceives Human Rationality." (2013).
33  Henrich, Joseph. *The Weirdest People in the World: How the West Became Psychologically Peculiar and Particularly Prosperous*. Farrar, Straus and Giroux, 2020.
34  Thompson, M. Guy. "Freud's Conception of Neutrality." *Contemporary Psychoanalysis* 32.1 (1996): 25–42.
35  Samuels, Robert. "Transference and Narcissism." *Freud for the Twenty-First Century*. Palgrave Pivot, Cham, 2019. 43–51.
36  Freud, Sigmund. *Totem and Taboo: Resemblances between the Psychic Lives of Savages and Neurotics*. Good Press, 2019.
37  Lacan, Jacques. *Transference: The Seminar of Jacques Lacan, Book VIII*. John Wiley & Sons, 2015.
38  Sartre, Jean-Paul. "Being and Nothingness." *Central Works of Philosophy v4: Twentieth Century: Moore to Popper* 4 (2015): 155.
39  Lehrer, Keith, and Carl Wagner. *Rational Consensus in Science and Society: A Philosophical and Mathematical Study*. Vol. 24. Springer Science & Business Media, 2012.
40  Leupin, Alexandre. *Lacan Today: Psychoanalysis, Science, Religion*. Other Press, LLC, 2004.
41  Samuels, Robert. "Logos, Global Justice, and the Reality Principle." *Zizek and the Rhetorical Unconscious*. Palgrave Macmillan, Cham, 2020. 65–86.

# Index

For Product Safety Concerns and Information please contact our EU
representative  GPSR@taylorandfrancis.com
Taylor & Francis Verlag GmbH, Kaufingerstraße 24, 80331 München, Germany

*9781032428604*